SABRINA FISHER REECE

How Do I Control My Emotions ?

When Anger, Rage and Impulsive Behavior is Destroying your Life

In59Seconds Publishing Co

First published by In59Seconds Publishing 2026

First edition

ISBN: 978-1-971622-12-5

This book was professionally typeset on Reedsy.
Find out more at reedsy.com

This book is for every man, woman and child that has lost control of their emotions. I know the pain behind these decisions very well. Do not give up on yourself. Each day presents a new opportunity for you to make a different choice. Love yourself enough to do the work needed to prevent anger and impulsive behavior from ruining your life. You Got This! You are worth the daily effort so please make it. Learning to think before you react will change your life for the better.

–Bri Reece

Contents

1

Only You - Can Control You

Believe it or not, I used to have a very bad temper. I used to brag and pride myself on having it. Overreacting to situations, ranting, and screaming to get my point across were normal behaviors for me. At the time, I wore my anger like a badge of honor. I believed it made me powerful. I believed it made me respected. I believed it made people listen.

I owned a famous, long standing braiding salon in Los Angeles called Braids By SaBrina, and as a business owner, I convinced myself that the only way to ensure my staff stayed in line and followed my rules was to rant and scream from time to time. I opened my salon at twenty six years old. I was silly and unskilled as a business owner. Whenever someone broke one of my very strict and detailed rules, I would explode. I would jokingly say it was because my astrological sign is Leo, which is said to be dominant and controlling. I leaned on that excuse heavily, as if the stars themselves had given me permission to behave however I wanted.

I lived that way for years. That worked for me to some extent but owning a business and governing over people is not just all business. In the hair business, you work very closely with people and you bond emotionally. As the boss of so many young women who were from similar backgrounds as me, I definitely came to think of some of them as family. I assumed a maternal roll in many of their lives. All the while still trying to heal from my past trauma.

At the time, I did not see my anger as a problem. I saw it as leadership. I saw it as authority. I saw it as passion. I confused intensity with effectiveness and control with strength. What I did not understand then was that fear and respect are not the same thing, and intimidation is not influence. However until I began my spiritual journey, that is how I operated.

Eventually, something inside of me began to shift. I started to recognize a very clear difference between people who followed rules because they respected me as their employer and people who followed rules because they were afraid me you, or afraid they would lose their job. The energy was different. The trust was different. The loyalty was different. I began to realize that love and kindness go a whole lot further than dictatorship ever could.

Still, awareness alone did not change me overnight. I didn't realize just how serious my issue with anger had become until I almost physically attacked one of my employees whose behavior had gotten terribly out of hand. That moment scared me, not because of what she had done, but because of what I was capable of doing. I had crossed an internal line I didn't even know existed.

In the end, my explosions were only hurting me. That hurt showed up in my life physically. I began to suffer from debilitating migraine headaches and severe stomach ulcers. I treated the symptoms with aspirin and other medications, never realizing that the treatment I actually needed to seek was internal. I was trying to heal externally what was being destroyed internally.

Anger is rarely just anger. It is often grief or hurt that has nowhere to go. It can be fear masked as dominance. Sometimes it is pain that was never processed. It is often a nervous system that has been in survival mode for far too long. I did not understand this then. I only knew how to react, not how to respond. I and writing this book so that, that realization comes sooner for others. No matter what we have been through or what someone has done to us, we are still responsible for how we react.

There will always be people who trigger anger in us. There will always be situations in life that have the potential to make us lose our temper. Regardless of how justified we feel in being mad, I now know that we are responsible for how we react to them. Most importantly, we can choose in that very moment exactly how we want to respond.

That realization changed my life. No one ever taught me how to regulate my emotions. No one ever modeled what emotional intelligence looked like. I grew up believing that loud meant strong and calm meant weak. I believed that if you did not dominate a situation, you would be dominated by it. Those beliefs did not come from nowhere. They were learned. They were conditioned, and they were reinforced through experience.

When you live in environments where chaos is normal, calm can feel unsafe.

3

So I stayed loud. Now let me be clear, the home I grew up in was not chaotic. It was my older sister and me, living with our grandmother and grandfather. From the time I was three months old until I turned seventeen, my life was stable. There was no constant drama, no instability, no daily fear. My grandmother was loving and kind. She taught us old-school Texas morals and values. She wanted us there. She treated my sister and me like her own children, not like the two abandoned girls left behind by her youngest son's woman.

And to be clear, my father did not abandon us, our mother did. My father lived in the home with us, though he struggled with alcoholism. He was never abusive. Despite the pain of knowing my mother was addicted and did not want us, my childhood itself was grounded, structured, and safe.

My real trauma did not begin until I was seventeen. That was the year my grandfather took the life of my grandmother, in front of me. That moment shattered everything I understood about safety, stability, and love. I believe that was the true source of my explosive behavior.

What I did not realize at the time was that every emotional explosion was training my body to stay in fight mode. My nervous system never learned how to rest. My mind was constantly scanning for danger. My body stayed braced for conflict, even when none existed. Over time, that internal stress began to wear me down.

Anger did not make me powerful. It made me sick. It took me years to understand that emotional control is not suppression. It is not pretending you are not angry. It is not swallowing your feelings until they poison you from the inside out. Emotional control is awareness. It is the pause. It is the ability to feel something deeply without allowing it to hijack your behavior.

4

Only you can control you.

That statement sounds simple, but it is one of the hardest truths to accept. We love to believe that people make us angry. That situations push us too far. That circumstances force our reactions. But the truth is, nothing and no one can make you behave a certain way without your consent.

Anger is information, not instruction. When we feel angry, we should stop in our tracks and take a deep breath before we proceed. When you feel it rise, it is telling you something needs attention. It is not telling you to explode. It is not telling you to lash out or to destroy relationships, opportunities, or your health.

Learning to pause was one of the hardest things I ever had to do. At first, the pause felt deeply uncomfortable. To be silent felt like weakness. Not reacting immediately felt unnatural, almost unsafe. I had spent so many years surviving as a little black girl from Compton, so that stillness felt foreign to my body. But with practice, I began to understand something powerful: the pause is where your power lives. The pause is where true choice exists, because in that space, you are in control. The pause is where you decide who you are going to be in that moment, whether you will react from habit or respond from intention.

Through that process, I had to relearn leadership. I had to relearn communication. I had to relearn how to feel anger without becoming it. I discovered that leadership is not about domination, volume, or fear, it is about clarity. It is about emotional regulation. It is about creating safety instead of tension. I had to accept that true strength is calm under pressure, not chaos under stress. The loudest person in the room is not always the strongest. Often, the strongest person is the one who remains grounded when everything around them feels unstable.

For a long time, anger had been running my life, and I had mistaken it for confidence. To be fair, I *was* confident. I was a cute little five-foot-two brown-skinned woman with a cute little figure, and I absolutely knew it. I carried myself with confidence on the outside. But baby, on the inside, I was a wreck. Beneath the poise and the presence lived unresolved pain, unprocessed trauma, and a nervous system that never felt safe. I looked strong, but I was exhausted and afraid. I appeared in control, but I was internally unraveling. That's when I realized that real confidence is not loud, it is regulated, rooted and stable. That stability began with learning how to pause.

As I began to do the internal work, my relationships started to change. My business environment shifted. People were no longer walking on eggshells. They were engaging and gravitating towards the me that was healing. They began to share their stories. They were growing, and so was I.

The greatest lie we tell ourselves is that our anger protects us. It does not. In reality, uncontrolled anger exposes us. It reveals our wounds. It highlights our lack of boundaries and it shows where healing is needed most. Once I stopped defending my temper, I could finally address it.

I learned that emotional maturity is not about never getting angry. It is about knowing what to do when you do. It is about understanding that your emotions are valid, but your behavior is your responsibility. bad behavior while angry can lead to unnecessary problems.

That lesson applies far beyond business.

It applies to relationships. Parenting. Friendships. Romantic partnerships. Everyday interactions. The way you respond when things do not go your way determines the quality of your life.

You cannot control people. Most often you can not even

control how they treat you. You cannot control certain circumstances. But you can always control yourself. I'm not saying it will be easy to do, but I am certain there would be far less people in jail if they stopped, took a breath and paused before they responded to someone they are angry with.

When you begin to master your reactions, your entire life changes. You stop apologizing for things you did not mean to say. You stop repairing damage that did not need to happen, and you stop carrying guilt for moments you wish you could redo.

Self control is self respect. Life is not happening to you. You are in control whether you want to accept it or not. Accepting it earlier in life can save you a world of trouble.

The moment I realized that my anger was destroying my health, my peace, and my credibility, I made a decision. I decided that no matter what someone else did, I would no longer give them control over my internal state.

That decision did not make me perfect. It made me aware, and awareness is where healing begins. I definitely understand that past trauma can cause deep internal pain that may cause people to act out but when you are in custody, they will not care what deep rooted problem you have that caused you to explode.

If you are reading this and recognizing yourself in my story, I want you to know something important. You are not broken or too emotional or overly dramatic. You may be valid in your reason for being angry. You simply learned survival tools that no longer serve you. Anger is misdirected energy. Learning to calm down and think will give you the opportunity to re-direct that energy in a positive way.

You can choose differently. You can become the calm presence you once believed was impossible for you. Your anger does not define you. how you choose to respond does.

7

Only you can control you, and the moment you accept that truth, you take your power back.

2

Anger is Not Your Friend

Anger is not your friend and it never will be. That is a hard truth to accept, especially in a world that often celebrates loud reactions, dominance, and emotional explosions as strength. For many of us, anger feels powerful. It feels protective. It feels like control. But over time, I learned that anger does not protect us. It isolates us. It does not give us power. It takes it away.

I know anger, I have met it head on personally. As a young woman I was misguided and confused. Alone in the world after my grandmother was taken away from me in a tragic way. I was trying to figure it out. there was no one to teach me about boundaries and how to pull back and take a breath when I felt overwhelmed with emotion. I quickly confused rage with standing up for myself, and that served no positive purpose in my life.

Aside from pushing away people that truly care about you, anger can and will cause severe mental and physical distress.

Research supports what many of us feel in our bodies but do not always connect to our emotions. Studies from the American Psychological Association show that chronic anger is linked to increased risk of heart disease, high blood pressure, stroke, digestive disorders, migraines, and weakened immune function. Anger also significantly increases anxiety and depression over time, even when it feels justified in the moment.

No matter how provoked we feel, we must take a second to take a deep breath and assess the current situation, then proceed with a consciously chosen response, as opposed to one that is reactive and impulsive. Think about everything first. Even if only for a second. That single second can save relationships, careers, reputations, and in some cases, lives.

Take a moment to consider the negative result of an explosive response. Rarely has anything productive ever come from responding out of anger. Anger causes us to hurt those we love and creates unnecessary distance in our relationships with others. It convinces us that being right matters more than being at peace.

I learned this lesson the hard way. I became severely over-whelmed with the challenges of running a business where I had to depend on others to perform to my standards and with the same work ethic I had. Over the years, so many girls worked for me, each one with a completely different personality, a different pace, a different level of consistency. And day after day, I carried the weight of my business on my shoulders, trying to hold everything together, trying to make sure it didn't fall apart.

I didn't realize how much pressure I had been internalizing until it started coming out as rage. It wasn't just "stress." It was years of holding things in, swallowing emotions, pushing through, and pretending I was okay because I had responsibilities. I was trying to be strong, trying to lead, trying to keep a roof over everyone's head—mine and theirs. And somewhere in the middle of all that, I stopped checking on the part of me that was silently breaking.

Because the truth is, I still never had the opportunity to heal from the loss of my grandmother. If I haven't already mentioned it, my beautiful grandmother, the one who raised me, was shot and killed in front of me by her husband of thirty-two years. I was only seventeen years old when that happened, and I had no idea how to heal from it. I just kept going, because that's what I thought you were supposed to do. But I still suffered from terrible nightmares from the day of the murder.

And there I was, trying to run a business while carrying all of that pain, trying to manage employees, solve problems, stay professional and composed, while I had all these unhealed wounds inside of me. I was building something on the outside, but on the inside, I was still that seventeen-year-old girl who never got a chance to breathe, grieve, or be held. Eventually, what I didn't heal started demanding to be felt.

One day, I held a staff meeting with nine of my employees. I wanted to address ongoing issues with tardiness, hygiene, and customer service. My business had been built on the quality of work I began doing in my home long before I ever opened my salon. I had poured everything I had into it. My name was on the door. My reputation was on the line. What I learned the hard way was how difficult it is to make other people care about your business the way you do.

At the time, my staff meetings consisted mostly of me dictating expectations and outlining consequences for breaking the rules. I believed leadership meant control. I believed fear would produce discipline. I believed being tough would keep everything in order. Although I would later learn to lead with a much calmer and softer approach, I had not learned that yet.

During this particular meeting, I made a conscious effort to address issues generally, without calling out any one person. I wanted to avoid finger-pointing. But one employee couldn't let it go. She kept interrupting, asking, *"Are you talking to me?"*

I had very little patience for this. I was constantly apologizing to clients and offering discounts to smooth things over when my staff made mistakes. It was my name on the building, which meant every error ultimately fell on me. That responsibility had been quietly building resentment inside of me for years.

Her name was Zelma, and I loved her dearly. She had a substance abuse problem that caused her behavior to be erratic at times. Ninety percent of the time, she was responsible, loyal, and dependable. But that other ten percent was fueled by unhealed wounds. We had a lot in common, and over the years, we had become like family.

That day, however, she wouldn't stop challenging me. She refused to accept the general reprimand like the rest of her coworkers. What made it worse was that she was often the one responsible for the very behavior I was addressing. I felt disrespected. Challenged. Undermined. And instead of pausing, I reacted.

If you've ever heard someone describe "seeing red," you would understand what happened next. In that moment, my vision narrowed until her face was the only thing I could see. It felt illuminated, almost glowing red, like a scene from a movie. Anger does that. Neuroscience shows that intense anger temporarily shuts down the prefrontal cortex, the part of the brain responsible for reasoning, impulse control, and decision-making. When anger takes over, we are literally not thinking clearly.

I reached for a small figurine statue that sat on my desk and motioned as if I were going to throw it at her head.

Then, suddenly, I stopped and that pause changed my life. I sat back down in my chair, trying to regain control, realizing I could have lost everything I had worked so hard to build in a single moment of rage. A business and my reputation, my freedom and my future. All of it could have disappeared because of one impulsive decision. just because of my inability to control my emotions. I did not have the knowledge I have not but thank God I stopped myself.

I took a deep breath and calmly told her she was fired. That moment terrified me. Not because of what she had done, but because of what I had almost done. No matter how angry someone made me, it was never acceptable for me to even consider hitting them. Anger had taken me somewhere I never wanted to go.

I knew immediately that I had a problem that needed to be addressed. In my desperation to regain control, I found an anger management coach named Dr. Young. his office was on Crenshaw Blvd in Los Angeles. He typically taught court-ordered group classes, but we agreed to six weeks of one-on-one anger management therapy at sixty dollars an hour.

That decision saved me. After completing those sessions, I enrolled in another anger management class at West LA College. I learned how to identify my triggers and how to interrupt my reactions before they took over. I learned that anger is often a secondary emotion, usually masking fear, hurt, shame, or exhaustion.

The stress of running a business, combined with my unresolved past trauma, had made my nervous system hyper-alert. Trauma research shows that when emotional wounds go unhealed, the body stays in survival mode. That means what feels like a minor inconvenience to someone else can feel like a serious threat to someone carrying unresolved pain.

This work helped me understand why my reactions were so explosive, but it also made something very clear: no matter the cause, I was still responsible for my response. That realization marked a turning point in my life. we are responsible for how we react. no matter what someone did to us. Responsibility does not mean blame. It means ownership. It means recognizing that even when anger is understandable, it is still destructive if left unchecked.

The next time you find yourself angry, slow down and give considerable thought to your reaction. Remember that there are truly good people sitting in a jail cell right now because of one impulsive moment. This will prevent you from overreacting and possibly becoming irate and exhibiting explosive behavior you will probably regret later.

Due to being committed to change, I have been able to identify certain things that serve as triggers for my temper and I try to avoid them at all cost. I never want to feel as out of control as I did that day.

Making the decision to voluntarily enter into anger management classes was one of the best decisions I have ever made. I had lived long enough as an angry person, and once I accepted why and who I was angry with I was finally able to make peace with it and move forward.

Anger is not your friend, and it never will be. It does not solve problems for you, it creates them. It will not command respect. On the contrary it breeds fear. It does not make you strong. It weakens your body, your mind, and your relationships.

You are not wrong for feeling anger. You are a human being. But you are responsible for what you do with it. The real strength is learning how to pause. The real power is learning how to choose peace over pride. True growth is learning how to respond instead of react.

Use these next few lines to list four things that you have identified as triggers for anger in your life.

(Example: When my teenage daughter doesn't clean up, when my staff comes to work late and does not address their tardiness, when someone walks out the room while we are in the middle of a conversation.)

1.
2.
3.
4.

Awareness is the first step. Change is the second. Peace is the reward. Anger is not your friend. But self control is.

3

Identify Your Issues

As time went on in my life I began to really unpack what I called "my issues". I used to say that phrase casually, almost jokingly, without fully understanding how serious it really was. My issues were not personality traits. They were not quirks. They were not just bad habits. They were unhealed wounds that had been shaping my reactions, my relationships, and my emotional world for years.

I soon came to realize a couple of the examples I listed were directly tied to my issues of abandonment and self worth. I would overreact to each of these situations every single time. There was no middle ground. No pause. No space to process. Just reaction. Big reaction. Emotional reaction. Defensive reaction. I did not understand then that when something feels bigger than the moment you are in, it usually is.

They triggered feelings of loss, disrespect and invalidation. Those feelings were not new. They were familiar. They lived deep inside of me, quietly waiting for opportunities to resurface. Whenever someone made me feel these emotions it triggered suppressed feelings I'd been harboring from my mother's abandonment and abuse. What looked like anger on the outside was actually fear. What looked like control was actually insecurity. What looked like rage was actually grief that had never been acknowledged.

Most importantly, it made me fearful that others would also disappoint and hurt me.

Fear has a way of disguising itself. It does not always announce itself clearly. Sometimes it shows up as defensiveness. Sometimes it shows up as sarcasm. Sometimes it shows up as distance. Sometimes it shows up as explosions. I had been responding to my fear for years without realizing that fear was driving the car.

It's important that we figure out why we respond negatively to certain situations so we can stop tormenting our friends and family with our unwarranted antics that they may not completely understand at the root. That sentence alone took me years to be able to say honestly. Because no one wants to believe they are the source of tension. No one wants to believe they are hurting people they love. But healing requires honesty, not perfection.

It is neither the fault of others that I didn't have the ideal parental relationship nor is it a given that I was destined to be hurt by others, but it would take years and a lot of work on myself before I realized that. That realization was freeing and terrifying at the same time. It was freeing because it meant I was not doomed to repeat the same emotional patterns forever. Terrifying because it meant I could no longer blame my reactions on everyone else. It meant responsibility landed squarely in my lap, and responsibility is heavy when you have been surviving instead of healing.

Identifying your issues is not about labeling yourself as broken. It is about becoming curious instead of critical. It is about asking

17

yourself hard questions without shame. It is about tracing emotional patterns back to their origin so you can finally stop reliving them in present-day situations.

Most of us react before we reflect. We feel first and ask questions later. Sometimes we defend ourselves before we understand ourselves. That is not because we are weak. It is because we were never taught how to sit with discomfort. We were never taught how to explore emotional triggers without judgment. We were taught to push through, toughen up, or lash out.

When you begin to identify your issues, you start noticing patterns. You notice that certain situations always make you feel the same way. You notice that certain people always seem to trigger the same response. You notice that your reaction is often bigger than the offense. That is your invitation to look deeper within yourself.

Your issues are not random. They are connected to moments when your needs were un-met, your voice was unheard, and possibly your safety was compromised. Until those moments are acknowledged, they will continue to speak through your behavior.

For a long time, I believed my reactions were justified because my feelings were real. What I had to learn was that feelings being real does not mean reactions are appropriate. Two things can be true at the same time. You can be hurt and still responsible for how you respond.

Healing begins when you stop asking, "Why do they keep doing this to me?" and start asking, "Why does this affect me so deeply?" That question changed everything for me. Once I began identifying my issues, I could finally separate past pain from present reality. I could see when I was reacting to someone in front of me versus reacting to someone from my past. I could tell the difference between actual disrespect and perceived rejection. I could slow down enough to choose a response instead of defaulting to a reaction.

This work is not easy. I can not promise it will be easy for you. But it will definitely be worth it. It takes deep internal work that requires sitting with emotions you have avoided for years. It requires acknowledging pain you have minimized and taking responsibility without self condemnation. It requires patience with yourself as you unlearn behaviors that once kept you safe.

But it is so worth it. Your life will change for the better. When you identify your issues, you reclaim your power. You stop bleeding on people who did not cut you. there is no more expecting others to heal wounds they did not create. You stop sabotaging relationships with unresolved pain.

You also begin to develop more compassion for yourself and others who act the way you used to. Instead of asking, "What is wrong with me?" you start asking, "What happened to me?" That shift changes everything. It moves you from shame to understanding and from blame to growth. You are no longer just surviving, you are healing. I did now always believe it, but healing is possible no matter what you have been through.

One of the most powerful things I learned is that awareness does not fix everything immediately, but it does give you choice. Choice is the foundation of emotional freedom. Be patient with yourself. Sit in silence and breathe deeply. Try to identify the areas of your life that you need to work on. Applaud yourself for being mature enough to notice those areas. You cannot heal what you refuse to name.

Identifying your issues does not mean you dwell in the past. It means you stop letting the past control your present. It means you stop reliving old pain in new situations. It means you stop reacting from wounds and start responding from wisdom.

This chapter is a call to action. I want you to pause before you react in any situation. Always stop and ask yourself what you are really feeling. Take a deep breath and notice when your emotions feel familiar. If the reaction that you are considering does not come from a place of love, peace and reason. do not do it.

Your friends and family deserve the best version of you. More importantly, you deserve peace. Healing does not mean you will never be triggered again. As long as you are alive and breathing life will present challenges. Healing means you will stop recognize the trigger and choose differently. It means you will interrupt the old cycle and choose something new. You will respond with awareness instead of impulse.

Your issues do not make you unlovable. They make you human being who is trying to be the best version of him or herself despite past trauma, hurt and the disappointments of life. Addressing those issue makes you brave.

When you identify your issues, you stop being controlled by them, and that is where real emotional freedom begins.

4

Spend Time with Your Mind

For us to become aware of our thoughts we first need to slow our lives down a bit. We must take advantage of quiet moments and be still long enough to monitor our thoughts. When you are sitting in traffic, turn the radio off, take a few deep breaths, and begin to notice and acknowledge every thought that comes into your mind. Learning to do this changed my life tremendously. Both good and bad thoughts need recognition. You cannot reverse negative thoughts if you have not taken the time to recognize and acknowledge they exist. Begin by keeping it as simple as taking a mental note of what you are thinking. Start by observing exactly what you are thinking right now. Take ten minutes and detach from everything in the world except your thoughts.

Make a conscious decision to do this every day and, eventually you will see the clear distinction between intentional thoughts versus when our mind runs rampant on its own without any guidance from us. Only then will you notice how many thoughts of fear and impending tragedy run through our minds. These are specifically the thoughts we must learn to dismiss. These are the thoughts that will ultimately cause us harm. It's not horrible to admit you have negative thoughts, on the contrary, it's the first step to a better life. Many will spend years in complete denial. Denying they are even capable of thinking negatively. Negative thoughts exist, just like crime, and while we may not be able to control the crime in the world, we have the power to monitor our thoughts. Stop judging your thoughts as good or bad and re-label them as "thoughts that make you feel good" or "thoughts that make you feel bad." Choosing to label them as good or bad will make you less likely to acknowledge the ones that are not in line with what you desire for your life. Denial and embarrassment will slow down the process. We all think negatively at times. No need to guilt yourself for being a bad thinker. We all have thoughts of fear, failure, anger, sickness, and sadness. You are not alone. You are not a bad person for thinking that way. However, now that you are aware of the damage sustaining a negative thinking pattern can do to your life, it's time to change it. Feel good about being at a place in your life where you are willing to make positive changes towards the betterment of your future. This is the best gift you can give to yourself and others. Learning how to control and change your thoughts will change your life. As human beings we can get so distracted by the ins and outs of our daily routines that most of us rarely even realize that we are thinking all day. Scientists say we have twelve to sixty thousand thoughts per day.

Thoughts come continuously, whether or not we choose to guide them. These thoughts are shaping our daily lives so we must learn to take charge of them. You are what you think all day long. There is no way around it. Our realities are shaped solely by our thoughts. If it's present in our lives, even if we don't remember those specific thoughts, we did indeed think them. We have to learn to create barriers to keep the negative thoughts from penetrating our subconscious mind. We can't avoid thinking, so it's best we take control over this imminent process and manipulate it in our favor. All thoughts travel on energetic frequencies. We are energy as well. Everything in this world is energy, and we have the power to control the energy we put out. Energy exists, no matter what, but we can determine if the energy we emit is positive or negative. If we are entertaining thoughts of disease because someone we know was just diagnosed with an illness and we are now in fear of getting it, then rest assured that our energetic vibration is low at that time.

The good thing is we are in control of the level of energy we put out. We can raise our own energetic vibration at any time. A friend of mine taught me about saging a few years ago. At that point in my life, I was open to new ideas and concepts regarding religion and spirituality. She brought a small piece of sage to my salon and showed me how to use it. I am a person that knows the importance of "belief" in something, so as she was showing me how to rid my body and private spaces of negative energy that can lurk in corners and dark spaces, I set a conscious intention to not reject what she was saying simply because it was foreign to me. Even though it was different and conflicted with my childhood Christian beliefs, I tried to listen and learn with an open mind. I decided that day that the practice of saging was no different than the Christian ritual of taking communion. The drinking of the grape juice and eating of the cracker is also a ritual in remembrance of Jesus Christ and his bodily sacrifice. Communion is a ritual that Christians chose to assign symbolism to. Unfortunately, it was my experience growing up in COGIC (Church Of God in Christ) that only our rituals were accepted, and everything else was considered voodoo or witchcraft. I no longer believe that. I can't say I ever personally bought into the voodoo concept; it was simply the belief of many of the elders that came before me. Most were devout Christians and would have never accepted the belief in healing crystals, burning sage and meditation to open our chakras. Chakras are the centers of spiritual power in the human body.

After my friend was gone I decided to practice what she taught me about saging. I also chose to envision the dark energy leaving through a window and the positive energy coming in. I would say "Negative energy out, positive energy in." As I walk around my salon burning the sage and setting my intentions for positivity and prosperity, I would close my eyes and believe it all as fact. What you believe is what truly matters. You can practice certain rituals but inside you have no faith in them, so they won't work. Many people believe the art of rituals and spiritual ceremonies are evil and demonic. My response to people who say that to me is "That's not what it means to me". Do not allow other people to assign an intention to something you choose to do. For example I am a mother of four and I would allow my children to dress up in customs for Halloween and take part in the parade at school. We would even go from house to house trick- or treating in the evening.

Frequently people have reminded me of some ancient original demonic meaning the Halloween holiday. It never bothered me one bit because that is not what me and my children celebrate it for. We have no evil intent behind our choice to celebrate the holiday nor are we bound by anyone else's. There is always someone who chooses to corrupt something. I choose to see the positive in all things. And any holiday that promotes love and brings people and families closer is OK with me. The choice to participate in something evil is just that, a choice. I'm not interested, and it has nothing to do with me.

The practice of saging became a regular practice in my salon, Braids By SaBrina, which has been my sole source of income for twenty-five years. In September 2019, I changed the name of my salon to "A New Vision Dreadlock Studio." One would think changing the name of a popular business that had serviced the Los Angeles community for so long would not be a great idea, but I sat in stillness for a while and the new name suddenly came to me in less than fifteen minutes. I was fifty years old.

I had recently dealt with some unexpected medical issues that caused me to rethink allowing any form of stress in my life. My staff at my salon were a key source of stress, and at this point there wasn't much of a financial benefit to keeping them around. I felt I had given all that I could to them over the years and now I had to make myself and my health a priority. I made an instant decision to terminate them and change the name of the salon to from "Braids By SaBrina" to "A New Vision Dreadlock Studio." It was a new day and time for A New Vision as I embarked upon the second half of my life. I operated that cute little purple studio for 10 years. I had peace and I made twice the money I made when I had the staff that caused me so much stress.

To this day, I have never regretted my decision. The new salon name came to me so peacefully that I knew it was God telling me to move forward. When we spend time with our mind we will discover answers to questions, solutions to problems will be revealed to us. I started sitting quietly in the empty salon; something I was never able to do when I had employees. I would visualize abundant wealth, and thank God for continued success. I spoke aloud words of gratitude for my business and how consistent it had been. Then I would walk from room to room, saging my beautiful purple salon and speaking my affirmations for both my business and myself aloud. I raised my personal prices considerably and within thirty days of re-branding my salon, I was making double what I made before, even without having a staff. It turned out to be one of the best decisions I have ever made.

Wealth and success can become a reality for anyone who sincerely believes it is possible. I believe that is why I have never experienced poverty. I expect wealth, and yes, I advertise and do all the footwork needed to sustain a small business, but that to me is secondary. My belief that the business could not fail was the primary cause of its continued success. Advertising and promoting a business won't work if subconsciously you believe it will fail. We must see the success in our mind first. God gave us this power as a gift to mankind, but most do not use it. You can experience success in all areas of your life if you first believe it to be possible. All things are possible!. This new practice of saging was just another tool I used to set intentions for peace and prosperity in my life.

There is not one specific tool. Any practice you put complete unwavering belief in will be successful. I'm pleased that I opened my mind and allowed myself to at least listen to other concepts and beliefs and make my own choices. Having that open mind allowed me to be more receptive when I traveled to Bali, Indonesia, Cusco, Peru, Cairo, Egypt, Istanbul, Turkey, and Athens, Greece. In these countries, I visited many monasteries and spiritual temples, which helped to strengthen my belief in one Divine Source.

Different people may package God differently. They may refer to God with a different name, but to me, it's all the same. I respect the amount of reverence that other countries give to honor the creator. I have partaken in many rituals and ceremonies that greatly differ from my Christian church practices. What I've learned is to allow others to worship God the way they choose. It's not my business. If there was a particular practice that resonated with me, I adopted it as my own and moved forward. I feel we get so distracted in pointing out the different way in which we all choose to acknowledge God.

Our ego wants us to be correct. It convinces us that our way is the only way. It's a distraction and a judgment that I don't believe in. To each his own. Who are we to say how another person should acknowledge God? The ultimate universal goal is to live a great life. Learning, growing and evolving in all areas and allowing others to do the same. I do, however, believe that once we fully evolve we don't necessarily need to practice daily rituals to remind us to be positive and speak positivity over our lives. By then, the positive thought process will have become second nature. However, until then, the daily practices that help us keep a positive mental attitude are crucial to having a productive life. They help us form positive daily habits. I was proud that I was able to open my mind and embrace practices that were a definite step out of the C.O.G.I.C. box I was raised in. I have gotten to a point where I enjoy them. I believe strongly in them. I believe they are necessary, and I look forward to doing them daily. I still believe very much in Jesus Christ. I believe he was here to teach us of our Amazing internal power.

I believe that power is what he was referring to as "The Kingdom of Heaven" with-in us all. I will always be eternally grateful for my Christian upbringing. Unlike most I see correlations between Christianity and spirituality. I combine what practices and beliefs work best for my life and move forward. I have convinced myself that taking that small time out of my day to speak positivity over my body, my family, my business, and my life in general is truly the reason I no longer suffer from many of the things a lot of people in this world currently suffer with. I want to teach others how I rid my life of sadness, pain, hopelessness and depression. I get so excited about teaching these practices to others because it is my desire for everyone to learn that their happiness is a choice, and choosing to spend just a little time with your mind can ensure you live a better life.

As far as we know, we only get one mind. Spend as much time with it as possible. View your mind as the cockpit of an airplane. With all the controls clearly accessible and you are the pilot.

Most people don't struggle because the cockpit is broken, they struggle because they're letting anything and everything grab the controls. A random thought becomes turbulence. A simple comment from someone becomes an alarm. Memories can cause storms within us. Then before they know it, they're flying on autopilot, reacting instead of choosing. But the truth is, your mind has instruments for a reason. You can check your altitude,how high or low your emotions are running. You can check your fuel, what type of mental and emotional fuel have you been feeding yourself all day: fear, stress, comparison, resentment... or peace, truth, gratitude, and self-love.

When you spend time with your mind, you start recognizing what every signal is trying to tell you. Sometimes anger is a warning light that you've been ignoring your limits. Anxiety can be your system telling you you're overloaded and need to slow down. When you feel sluggish, is your body asking for rest and release?. Feelings of sadness can mean its time to do a internal self check. You don't have to panic just because a light flashes, you simply have to learn what it means, and respond like a controlled and efficient pilot, not like a frightened passenger.

28

Because passengers don't control the flight, they just endure it. Pilots stay present. Pilots make adjustments. Pilots don't jump out of the plane when the wind gets rough; they grip the controls, steady the aircraft, and fly through it with wisdom and love. That is what emotional maturity looks like: not a life without turbulence, but a life where you know how to keep your hands on the controls when turbulence shows up.

5

Putting That Old Story To Rest

There comes a moment in life when you realize that the pain you keep tripping over is not always coming from the present. Sometimes it is coming from a story you have been telling yourself for years. A story that once helped you survive, but no longer serves who you are becoming.

For a very long time, I identified as an abandoned child. I referred to myself as broken. I was the girl whose mother tried to throw her away. I was the unwanted child who witnessed the murder of the grandmother who raised her. I carried those truths with me everywhere I went, not just as memories, but as identity. I did not realize how deeply that story had woven itself into the way I saw myself, the way I interpreted other people's behavior, and the way I moved through the world.

No one was walking up to me on the street reminding me of what I had been through. No one was stopping me mid conversation to say, "Remember, you were abandoned by your mom," or "Remember, you lost your grandmother, the who loved you most to tragedy." That wasn't happening. What was happening was much quieter and much more dangerous. I was reminding myself.

I was replaying the old story. I was reviving it in my mind. I was activating it when normal life situations would happen. If a relationship ended or I experienced some other form of disappointment. I was reaching for it whenever I felt unseen, unheard, or unsupported. Without realizing it, I was using my past as proof for my present pain. Every moment of silence felt like abandonment. Every loss felt like confirmation that nothing ever stays. All unmet expectation felt like rejection to me all over again.

The story became my lens. I honestly didn't know any better. It was my story, my truth. The problem with living through an old lens is that it distorts the present. It makes you respond to today as if you are still standing in yesterday's trauma. You feel unsafe even when you are not. You find yourself bracing for impact even when there is no threat.

For years, I thought I was being honest about my life by retelling my story. Especially since I had initially suppressed it. I thought that finally acknowledging my pain meant constantly revisiting it. I thought that honoring my grandmother meant living forever in the grief of losing her. I felt that acknowledging my abandonment meant staying connected to it emotionally and as they say "Owning my truth." What I did not understand was that I had crossed the line between honoring my past and living inside it.

At some point, survival stories become cages. There is a season where identifying what you have been through is necessary. Naming trauma can be powerful and acknowledging your pain is essential to healing. But there is another season where continuing to live from that identity keeps you stuck. I did not realize how often I was unconsciously introducing myself

31

to the world as a wounded person, even when my life no longer reflected that reality. I had a successful career as a motivational speaker. I spoke on over 40 stages and was blessed to motivate and encourage many people who had be through similar traumas. I do not regret my years as a speaker but I do remember how emotionally exhausted I would be after I got off stage.

Speaking motivationally showed me that there are a lot of hurt people in this world. many have no clue that healing is even possible. Many people think just like I did, that they will be dealing with the residue of past trauma for the rest of their lives.

I was a grown accomplished and resilient entrepreneur. I was loved by many. I had built businesses. I had raised children. I had employed and helped thousand of women. I had survived what should have destroyed me. Yet emotionally, part of me was still standing in the moment of loss, waiting for someone to save me again. Parts of me still felt unworthy and that feeling brought out anger in me.

That realization that i was still, even by age forty, dealing with the things that hurt me as a child was painful. Because it meant that some of my suffering was no longer being caused by what happened to me, but by what I kept telling myself about what happened to me. It meant I had to confront the fact that I was the one reopening wounds that were trying to heal. I was feeding pain that was asking to be released.

I had to ask myself a very uncomfortable question. Who would I be without this story? I truly did not know and that terrified me. As horrible as it all was, but did I have an identity without it?

When you have lived so long identifying with survival, letting go of that identity can feel like betrayal. It can feel like you are minimizing what you went through or dishonoring the people you lost. It can feel like you are pretending things did not happen. But putting the old story to rest is not denial. It is not disrespectful, it is growth and integration. That is where healing begins.

Choosing to heal from those old hurtful stories is saying, "This happened to me, but it does not get to define me forever." I had to learn the difference between remembering and reliving. Remembering allows you to extract wisdom. Reliving keeps you trapped in pain. Remembering honors your journey. Reliving keeps you emotionally frozen in time.

For a long time, I did not realize how often I was reliving instead of remembering. Of course when I would tell my story to audiences on stage I had to relive it but in other situations I would noticed it in how deeply certain disappointments cut me. I noticed how quickly I felt abandoned when people did not show up the way I hoped they would. How easily I interpreted neutral behavior as rejection. That was not the present speaking. That was the old story talking.

The abandoned child inside of me was still trying to protect herself. But I am not that child anymore. That truth was both liberating and heartbreaking. Because it meant I had to grieve something new. I had to grieve the identity I had built around my pain. I had to let go of the comfort that came with familiarity, even when that familiarity was causing me to continue suffering.

Putting the old story to rest required me to sit with emotions I had been avoiding. It required me to stop blaming the world for wounds I had not yet healed. It required me to take responsibility for how often I was reopening chapters that had already ended.

That was not easy for me to do. There were days when I

felt like I was betraying my younger self by choosing to move forward. There were moments when I felt guilt for not carrying my pain as heavily as I once did. Sometimes were moments when I questioned whether healing meant forgetting. It does not. I could never forget my amazing country grandmother from Dallas Texas. Everything good about me is from being raised by her.

I had to learn that I could love my grandmother deeply without living in the trauma of losing her. I learned that I could acknowledge my mother's abandonment without continuing to abandon myself. I eventually learned that I could tell my story without letting it tell me who I was allowed to be. I was able to speak about my past without being emotionally debilitated after.

The old story served a purpose once. It helped me survive. It helped me make sense of pain I did not choose. It helped me understand why I was the way I was. But survival is not the same as living. At some point, the tools that help you survive will prevent you from thriving if you do not lay them down.

Putting that old story to rest did not happen overnight. It happened in small moments of awareness. Moments where I caught myself spiraling and gently redirected my thoughts. Moments where I chose compassion instead of self pity. There were moments where I reminded myself that I was safe now.

That word became important to me. Safe. Safe does not mean nothing bad will ever happen again. Safe means you trust yourself to handle whatever does. Safe means you are no longer living as if the ground is constantly about to disappear beneath you. It means you are present in your life instead of bracing for loss.

I had to practice telling myself a new story. A story where

34

I was not defined by what was taken from me, but by what I built. I was not broken, I was resilient. A story where I was not abandoned, but chosen by my own commitment to myself.

That shift changed everything. When I stopped reviving the old story, my relationships changed. My reactions softened and my expectations became healthier. I stopped looking at people as potential abandoners and started seeing them as human beings with their own limitations. I stopped internalizing every disappointment as a reflection of my worth.

I began to feel lighter. Putting the old story to rest did not erase my pain. It transformed it. It turned it into wisdom. It was turned into empathy, compassion and purpose. It allowed me to use my experiences to help others without drowning in them myself.

There is a difference between carrying your story and being carried by it. One gives you strength. The other steals it from you.

If you are honest with yourself, you may recognize moments where you are still reviving an old story. Maybe yours is abandonment or rejection like mine. Maybe it is betrayal or the fear of it. It could be not feeling chosen. Whatever it is, ask yourself whether that story is still true in the present moment or whether it is simply familiar to you.

Familiar pain is not the same as current danger. You are allowed to update your identity and become better and stronger. You are allowed to evolve beyond what hurt you. You can put down the weight of who you had to be to survive and step into who you get to be now.

Putting that old story to rest is not forgetting. It is forgiveness. It is compassion. It is choosing to stop punishing yourself for what you did not deserve.

The child in you survived. The adult in you gets to live and that is not betrayal. That is healing. The healing that we all deserve.

This chapter is an invitation to notice when you are replaying a story that no longer reflects who you are. An invitation to gently close chapters that have already taught you what they needed to teach you. This is an invitation to stop introducing yourself to the world through pain that has already shaped you.

You are more than what happened to you. You are a phenomenal creation of God. You always have been.

When you are ready to put that old story to rest, you create space for a new one. One written from wholeness, not wounds. One written from strength, not survival. One written from truth, not trauma.

6

Take A Breath With Bri

For most of my life, I believed strength looked like immediate response. If something hurt me, I reacted. If something angered me, I exploded. If something felt unfair, I spoke up instantly, loudly, and with conviction. I thought hesitation meant weakness. I thought pausing meant losing control of the narrative. I thought silence meant surrender. What I did not understand yet was that the pause is not where power disappears. The pause is where power is born.

When you grow up without all the love you deserved you learn to respond quickly. you always think someone is trying to take more away from you. You learn to scan rooms for danger. You are always attempting to protect yourself before anyone else has the chance to hurt you. My nervous system was trained early to stay alert, reactive, and ready. I did not know how to slow down because slowing down once meant being unsafe. My body learned to equate speed with survival. So when something triggered me, my reaction felt automatic. My mouth moved before my mind caught up. My emotions took the wheel before my wisdom could even sit in the car. Bottom line, I had absolutely no control over my emotions.

For a long time, I justified my impulsive behavior by calling it passion. I told myself I was just expressive. I told myself people needed to hear the truth, even if it came out sharp. I believed if I did not speak up immediately, I would be silenced. But the truth is, I was not reacting from clarity. I was reacting from fear. Fear of being dismissed or devalued again. Fear of being overlooked or disrespected. Fear of being abandoned again. This is why I wrote this book. Sometimes reactive, explosive people have so much going on inside of them that causes that behavior. I am not making excuses for bad behavior. I simply want you to understand the importance of getting to the root of what has caused the pain. the fear, the disappointment so that you can fix it.

There is a very small space that exists between a trigger and a reaction. That space is so small that most people never notice it. They go straight from emotion to explosion without realizing there was another option available to them. I lived there for years, skipping over that space like it did not exist. Until one day, I realized that every regret I had ever carried lived in the moments where I did not pause. Stopping and simply taking a breath can make all of the difference in the world.

Every argument that escalated unnecessarily. Relationship that fractured beyond repair or opportunities that dissolved because I said something I could not take back. Every moment I wished I could rewind. They all had one thing in common. I did not pause and take that breath.

The pause does not mean you are wrong. It does not mean you are weak or afraid to speak. It means you are choosing to respond instead of react. It means you are allowing your higher self to enter the conversation. You are deciding that peace matters more than proving a point. Took me a long while to get there but I did and so can you. I got tired of being the one everyone expected to go off. My going off was not always screaming. Sometimes it was extremely dramatic crying fits.

Learning to pause was uncomfortable for me at first. Silence felt foreign. It felt like standing naked without armor. It felt like I was letting someone think they had the upper hand. But what I learned was this: when I paused, I was not giving my power away. I was reclaiming it. I was intentionally choosing how to respond.

That small pause gave me time to ask myself important questions. Is this worth my energy? Is this reaction aligned with the woman I am becoming? Is this situation about the present moment, or is it waking up something old inside of me? Am I responding to what was said, or am I responding to how it made me feel about myself? These are vital questions we all should ask ourselves when we feel triggered. Those questions changed my life and they will change yours too.

I began to notice how many situations were not actually emergencies. They only felt urgent because my emotions were loud. I noticed how often I mistook discomfort for danger. At times my reactions were rooted in old pain rather than current reality. The pause and the deep breath helped me separate what was happening now from what had happened before.

There is power in realizing that not everything requires an immediate response. Some things require reflection. A lot of things require distance. Many things require prayer and stillness. Sometimes you need to sleep on it. Allow some things time to settle in your spirit before they ever leave your mouth.

I had to learn that my worth does not diminish if I do not respond right away and loudly. Silence does not mean agreement. Pausing does not mean approval. It means discernment. It means emotional maturity. Intentionally choosing long-term peace over short-term relief.

Because reacting feels relieving in the moment. It feels like release and like you won. It feels like standing up for yourself. But relief is not the same as healing. Impulsive expression is not the same as resolution. Most often you feel worse afterwards.

I used to believe that if I did not say something immediately, the moment would pass and I would lose my chance to be heard. What I eventually learned is that when something truly needs to be addressed, it will still be there after you pause and think about it. When something does not survive the pause, meaning once you have paused and took a deep breath and thought about it and you find it is not as serious as you thought, then it probably did not deserve the reaction in the first place.

Learning to pause and take a breath taught me that my emotions are messengers, not masters. They are meant to inform me, not control me. Feeling angry does not mean I have to act angry. Feeling hurt does not mean I have to lash out at others. If I am feeling triggered that does not mean I have to explode.

There is power in breathing before speaking. There is power in walking away temporarily and sitting still for a moment. It's honorable to stop and let your nervous system calm before engaging. There is respect in choosing wisdom over impulse.

As I practiced pausing and breathing, I noticed something surprising. People treated me differently. Conversations shifted and arguments softened. My presence felt steadier and calm and my words carried more weight because they were not thrown around recklessly. When I did speak, it was clear and thought through. It was grounded. I was intentional with my words, so

40

nothing slipped out that i did not plan to say.

Learning to pause first gave me access to my own intuition. That quiet inner voice that had always been there but was often drowned out by extreme emotions. When I slowed down, I could hear it again. I knew that somethings were not worth my time. I sensed when silence was more powerful than speech. I could tell the difference between something that needed to be addressed and something that needed to be released. Learning that type of control is will change your life for the better.

I stopped reacting to everything as if it were a threat. I no longer gave my emotional energy to situations that did not deserve it. I stopped letting other people dictate my internal state. Even at times when people were down right wrong, which can truly upset you, but I still paused and took my breath first.

The pause taught me that I do not have to attend every argument I am invited to. Nor do I have to explain myself to people who are committed to misunderstanding me. I do not have to defend my growth to people who benefit from my chaos.

Pausing allowed me to grow without announcing it. To heal without performing and to change internally without asking permission. The true healing starts from the inside.

There is something incredibly powerful about choosing calm when you have every reason to react. It is not suppression. It is self mastery. Which is something I was every reader of this book to develop because you are indeed the master of your own fate.

I am not saying the pause is easy. Trust me it is not. It may feels like holding your breath or biting your tongue. Sometimes it feels like pushing down words that want to come out. It can feel like resisting the urge to prove yourself. But every time you pause and take that breath you strengthen a muscle inside of you. You master self-control and emotional intelligence. It will get easier and soon you will be so proud of yourself.

Over time, the pause becomes natural. It becomes instinct and second nature. You will stop reacting because you no longer need to protect a wounded version of yourself. You will be able to maturely respond from a healed place, a secure place and grounded place. that is the ultimate goal for anyone who has had a hard time controlling their emotions.

Learning this helped me stop reliving my past in the present. It helped me stop responding to people as if they were my mother, my hurt, my abandonment, my pain. It helped me see people for who they were, not what they triggered in me.

There is power in knowing that you always have a choice. Even when emotions rise you still have a choice. Even when someone is dead wrong, you can still choose how you respond to them. Even when your thoughts spiral out of control. You can pause and take a deep breath. You can think for a moment and choose differently.

This is where healing and transformation happens. It is where old patterns lose their grip and new more productive responses are born. This is when you step out of survival and into self-leadership.

You do not lose yourself in the pause. You find yourself. The new you The more you practice it, the more easier it is to accomplish it. You begin to realize that being peaceful is not passive. It is being smart. Maintaining peace is powerful and it gives you the control over any situation.

We are all powerful human beings. Once you learn to access that power and use it in a positive way, your life will never be the same.

That is why, when I create my inspirational videos for YouTube, TikTok, and Instagram, I always begin the same way. I begin with a pause and a deep breath. I begin with an invitation for my listeners tune back into the body, back into the moment, back to a calm place.

I say, *"Take a breath with Bri."*

And we stop.

And we breathe together deeply.

Then I say, *"Take a breath with Bri, and you will see... that everything is going to be alright."*

Because it is.

When you take the time to learn how to control your emotions, you stop letting the moment control you. You stop handing your power to triggers, memories, and impulses. You begin responding from intention instead of instinct. You begin choosing peace instead of chaos.

The fact that you are here, reading this, reflecting, doing the work, means you are already on the correct path. You are taking responsibility for your inner world. You are learning to pause. You are learning to breathe. You are learning to lead yourself.

So take a breath with me. Right here. Right now. Because when you learn to pause... When you learn to breathe... When you learn to choose instead of react...Everything truly is going to be alright.

7

I Declare War

In the previous chapter I speak about having had a very bad temper for many years. We exert so much energy in our confrontations and disagreements with other people. We can get so mad over differences of opinion. When we feel offended or disrespected we feel compelled to "set that person straight," even if doing so requires screaming and exerting extremely negative behavior, which can in turn destroy the relationship. We will declare war on some people and vow never to speak to them again as a punishment. We make enemies and will spend hours having imaginary conversations where we give them a piece of our mind, getting ourselves so upset that we cause permanent wrinkles in our forehead.

These external enemies receive all of our attention thus affecting us physically, mentally and emotionally. It consumes so much of our mind space that it can become a huge distraction. It can prevent us from advancing in all areas of our lives. I believe if we declare that same war on our internal enemy, our lives will improve for the better.

If we take all of that energy and us it to work on ourselves so that we can be better people it will not be energy lost and our lives will greatly improve.

Your internal enemy is that little voice in your head that tells you that you can't or are incapable of achieving something. When you are upset, it is that internal enemy that tell you to scream and holler or act out violently. I call this inner enemy "mind chatter" and it can lie to us and prevent us from realizing our true potential. This voice has controlled many of us for years. Many people are unaware of this voice. On the contrary, there are others who have recognized the voice, some religious folk even refer to the voice as "the devil' or " The Prince of Lies," yet still have not gained the power to not be affected by the its negative rantings.

Many philosophers refer to the voice as "The Ego". In my opinion, it does not matter what name you call the voice in your head, as long as you realize that everything it tells you is not the truth and you have the power to override all of the negative chatter and replace it with positive self talk. For those prone to impulsive behavior, learning to identify the negative mind chatter will help you to maintain control of your emotions.

The internal voice is a product of your subconscious mind. It is fueled by your fears and doubts until you learn to reprogram it. In this book I offer techniques that will assist you in repro-gramming and officially declaring war on that negative voice in your head.

Declaring war and effectively winning that war with the enemy of the mind should be the ultimate goal. If the war is won with-in you, all external enemies won't even have the ability to affect you. The true battle is in the mind. Gaining the abilities to control your thinking patterns and learning to master control of our thoughts will allow you the privilege of only accepting thoughts that serve you well into your mind space and you will develop the ability to cast out negative thoughts and images because they are the true internal enemy. Mastering this will prevent extreme behavior. You will stop, breath and make a choice to reject any thoughts that are telling you to explode and act out. This will give you time to be still and intelligently decide how you want to respond to any given situation.

It all truly does begin in the mind. Maintaining a persistent negative thinking pattern will prove to be more harmful to you than anything you can ever encounter in your life. Before people scream, lash out or become violent there is a thought and split second of a thought to do so. We have the power to dismiss certain thoughts and restructure our mind in that moment. We must learn the tools needed to declare all out war on anything that prevents us from leading a happy fulfilling life, and anger, rage and impulsive behavior threaten your livelihood.

This is one of the main reasons why I felt compelled to write this book. It is my desire to share with the world the tools that helped me change my negative mindset.

The first step in changing self-deprecating internal dialogue is identifying it. What has the enemy of the mind been repeatedly saying to you? What has the internal enemy convinced you of that simply is not true?.

Please list four things that you may not say out loud but you repeat them internally. List phrases that you say to yourself that make you hurt, sad or angry.

(Example: "Most women in my family develop breast cancer, I'm probably next." "No one at my new job likes me." "Bill disrespected me, I am going to tell him off," "I'll never find someone who truly loves me.")

46

I DECLARE WAR

1.

2.

3.

4.

8

We Choose to Suffer

Many horrible things have happened to so many people through-out their lives. A huge amount of us have endured trauma, abuse, death and disappointment. Some incidents have been so horrendous we do not feel we can ever move forward.

I may know I mentioned this story earlier but here is the extended version. When I was seventeen years old, less than thirty days away from my high school graduation, I personally witnessed a tragedy that changed my life forever.

My grandfather, grandmother, her youngest son who was my father, my sister and I lived in a large home in Compton. It had three gigantic bedrooms, a full size kitchen and service porch. There was a large separate living room and dining room, a long hallway, two bathrooms, and a massive backyard with a huge avocado tree. The property had another smaller home in the back that my father's sister SaBra (who I was named after) lived.

We were happy, healthy children, very well taken care of by our grandmother.

My grandparents were both born in Dallas, Texas and were poor growing up as children, so they were determined to make sure they never experienced lack once they moved to California. We always had more than enough food. There was a large, deep freezer in our home that they kept stocked with food.

Quite often my grandmother would tell us stories of her childhood in Texas. She would tell us that she could take a quarter and buy and loaf of bread and a slab of salami. She told us so many stories of having only one pair of shoes and having to walk from North Dallas to South Dallas to school everyday. Looking back, I wish I would have paid more attention to those priceless stories.

My grandmother my older sister Mary and myself in the front yard
of our home on 126th st in Compton

My grandfather and grandmother did not have any children together. They met in Dallas after my grandmothers divorce from her first husband Charlie Fisher.

My sister and I were the only two children of her youngest son, so when our mother couldn't take care of us due to her drug addiction, my grandmother gladly took over. My sister and I were infants, only 11 and 3 months old when she took us into her home. She was sixty-nine years old and had already raised three children of her own. I'm sure the decision to take on children that most likely were born with drugs in their systems could not have been an easy one, but she did it wholeheartedly and willingly.

My grandfather was not the biological father of my grandmother's three children. He was her second husband who had moved her and her children to California from Dallas to give them a better life.

My grandmother didn't speak a lot about their relationship when we were children, but it was always clear to us even as small kids that he was not the love of her life. He was simply a nice man who was a great provider who moved her and her children from Dallas to California in the 1950's. I never knew my grandmother to work her husband was the sole provider in our household.

Although our grandfather lived in the home with us for the entire seventeen years my sister and I were there, I don't remember having a lot of personal interaction with him. I have no memory of any parental advice at all. I can clearly remember my father and my grandmother taking time to talk to and teach us things as we grew up but I don't ever remember my grandfather talking to us or telling us stories. In retrospect I find that unusual but it was just normal to us back then. I also don't recall having a need or urge to bond with him either.

He cut grass for a living so there were always large lawn mowers in our home. The only outfit I ever remember him wearing was a pair of green overalls. His legal name was McClendon Fair but we all called him Mack. He was a tall man, at least 6 foot 3 inches. I can't say for sure if he was soft spoken, I can only say that I don't have any real memory of what his voice sounded like. He spoke to us so rarely. He definitely never yelled at us or my grandmother. I don't even remember ever hearing them argue.

My last year of high school, I was alone in my room when my grandmother came into my room with a concerned look on her face. I was laying on my bed and she stood there with her hands on her hips with a worried look. She said, *"Mack said he was gonna kill me."* She seemed worried but, like I said I had never witnessed him abuse or even raise his voice at her our entire childhood.

Being raised in the church, I was taught that prayer fixes everything. I responded and said to her *"Well Mama, if you know where he keeps the gun then please go take it and remove the bullets."* Once she left my room I got onto my knees and prayed, *"God, Mama doesn't seem happy. I love her, please make her happy."*

The next day was Sunday, May 3, 1997. I was only 17 years old but I was in a committed relationship with a young man who would later become my first husband. He worked as a security guard and was coming to pick me up one day after his shift. I was aimlessly walking through the house from room to room to pass the time until he arrived.

I went into my grandparents room which was a very large bedroom that had been added onto the home. It was the size of a large living room. I walked into their room and immediately noticed a gun laying on the television stand. I instantly reflected back to the conversation my grandmother and I had the day before when I had told her to remove the bullets from the gun. I walked over to the gun and picked it up. Only because of my boyfriend's profession and the fact that he carried a 357 magnum himself which he had recently demonstrated the workings of did I know how check the gun to see if my grandmother had indeed removed the bullets like I suggested to her the day before.

I picked up the gun, opened the cylinder, noticed that the bullets were still in the gun. I slowly started to turn the gun downward and allow the six bullets to slide out of the cylinder and into the palm of my hand. Instantly I thought, *"SaBrina you are being silly, they have been married for thirty-two years"* So I stopped just as the bullets were half way out and i turned the gun upward and let the bullets slide back into the gun. The gun was so old and rusty I was afraid to pop the cylinder closed.

My grandmother and grandfather were both in the kitchen. I walked onto the service porch, which is next to the kitchen, and said to my grandfather as I held the gun with the open cylinder in my left hand. I said *"I opened your gun, but I'm afraid to close it."* He was sitting in his normal seat at the kitchen table and my grandmother was standing directly across from him. He looked up at me and responded, *"What are you doing with my gun? Do not play with guns!"* I replied, *"Clyde taught me how to open it."* Clyde was my current boyfriend.

My grandfather got up from the table and took the gun out of my hand and sat back down at the table. He sat the gun on the kitchen table and continued to lecture me about gun safety.

Instantly, my grandmother who was still standing picked up the gun and immediately turned it away from both of us pointing in the direction of a window that was behind her. She began to refer to the weight of the gun, she bounced it up and down saying *"This gun is heavy, Verie (who was a relative of hers) has a gun like this."* As soon as her hand came down from the bouncing, the gun went off behind her under the window. The startling sound caused me to run, but I heard my grandfather say to her, *"You tried to kill me."* I could hear his kitchen chair scraping the floor as he pushed back. I stopped and immediately returned to the doorway of the kitchen in time to see my grandfather remove the gun from my grandmother's hand and shoot her in the head.

Things appeared to be moving in slow motion. It seemed as though I saw the hole begin to form in my grandmothers head. I saw her body slowly begin to slump and fall to the ground. I believed I would be next, so I turned and ran through the house and out the front door. I kept running until I got six doors down to a neighbor's home. This was the house of childhood friends we had grown up with, Reuben, Lavonne and Craig (who would later become KAM, the famous rapper from Compton).

I ran up to the door and began to beat on the door hysterically. Someone opened the door and I began to scream, *"My grandfather killed my grandmother!"*

I'm not sure if I blacked out after that, but when I returned outside from their house the streets were blocked and there were loud sirens, it seemed like utter chaos. My entire world changed that day. Life as I knew it would never be the same.

I have carried the memory of that tragic day with me for years. I have replayed that memory over and over in my head for what felt like a lifetime. I re-traumatized myself with the visual images of my grandmothers lifeless body falling to the floor after being shot in the head by my grandfather, her husband of 32 years.

Although this happened when I was a child, I held this horrible memory in my mind for years and I suffered from it well into my late 40s. I had nightmares of that day for decades. The scene of her death played like a movie in my mind repeatedly. I had come to terms with the fact that I would forever be plagued with this memory and the pain of this devastating day.

I have since learned that despite the tragedy of the incident,

WE CHOOSE TO SUFFER

my lifelong suffering from it is still a choice. This can be a hard concept for people to grasp. No one wants to believe that they had anything to do with their own continued suffering. Meaning: This was a horrible thing to experience. But lets just say I lost control and hit someone or acted out in some impulsive way and got arrested. Do you think the police or the justice system will care about my story? Will they care that I witnessed and murder and be lenient with me? Absolutely not. No matter what you have been through in life, you still must learn to maintain control over yourself and your behavior.

I don't mean to sound cruel or insensitive. I simply want you to know how vital it is to learn to control yourself, even while you are still healing.

Suffering is a choice.

What I witnessed was traumatic and no child should ever have to see the slaughter of anyone let alone a loved one. After years of replaying the day in my head, I have come to realize that that day has long passed and I do not have to revisit it. Doing so has caused years of suffering which negatively affected my mental and physical well being. I had no idea I could choose to stop replaying that horror movie in my head. Once I learned to press "stop" instead of "play" my suffering began to subside.

Just because we experience pain does not mean we have to endure that pain for the rest of our lives. We must learn the tools to eject those negative thoughts and images that cause us so much pain. Continuing to suffer from past trauma is a conscious choice. We must make peace with our past and eventually turn the movie off. It can be hard for people to accept that we choose to replay the past.

"Past trauma creates changes in our lives that we don't get to choose. Healing is about creating change that we <u>can</u> choose."

We can choose how we show up in the world. It is up to us even in the midst of hurt and pain, we still must maintain full control. I know how bad the pain of life can be. I urge any of you reading this to take the steps needed to heal from the inside so that that hurt and pain does not spill over onto the outside.

We are doing a disservice to ourselves by not allowing ourselves to move forward emotionally. Staying stuck in the pain of the past can be a detriment to our lives. We must cast out these memories and make a conscious choice not to relive them.

Visualize past traumatic memories like a speeding tennis ball headed straight toward you, but now you have the racket and the ability to not let the tennis ball hit you as it has so many times in the past. Stand strong and swat the tennis ball away aggressively, hit the ball so hard it flies up and over into the atmosphere, so far away that it disappears and never returns.

This visualization technique sincerely helped me to stop allowing bad memories into my present. I was able to cast out the memory every time it entered my mind. Realizing that I had a choice in the matter was very empowering. I learned that I had the control over my own life and I could choose not to continuously torment myself.

Use my tennis ball and racket visualization technique to gain control over your past negative memories or use the next few lines to create one that is specifically designed for you.

1.

2.

3.

4.

I have another visualization technique that helps me feel safe when I am driving. I used to drive a very large truck, a hummer H2, for ten years and I always felt safe. When I changed to a much smaller car that was lower to the ground I found myself experiencing a lot of anxiety whenever I would drive. I was fearful that I would get into an accident and because the car was so small I would not survive it. I know the danger of allowing fearful thoughts to persist in your mind, so I created a visual of my little silver car wrapped in a protective bubble. I convinced myself that this bubble was impenetrable and that it would protect me and my children as we rode in the vehicle.

The mind is such a powerful tool. More powerful that we can

even imagine. Whatever we train our mind to believe becomes reality. If you are struggling with hurt, pain, trauma etc that shows up as anger, rage, impulsive behavior or erratic emotions please seek help so that you can enjoy a peaceful life. Stop saying "I have a bad temper" or "There is no fixing me" or "I will never heal from this" Yes you can and yes you will. But you have to be willing to do the work.

"It is done unto you as you believe."
-Matthew 9:29-

We cause ourselves a lot of unnecessary suffering by choosing to hold onto unfounded beliefs. We speak words over our lives that do not represent the person we want to be. You will not drown in hurt forever. You are not a angry person. You will not destroy your life because you can't control your emotions. You are a wonderful, fully capable human being that is now taking full control over your life.

9

Closing Our HOLES

By the second half of my life, I had learned many tools to control my emotions and to keep myself calm, uplifted and positive. I had read hundreds of self-help books and completely transformed my life from a depressed, angry woman who felt let down by the abandonment of my mother into a confident mother, business owner, artist, author, and positive leader in my community.

I was born to two substance abusers. My mother had a vice for drugs, while my father had a vice for alcohol. My mother was cold, loveless, and abusive, but my father was not. He loved both my older sister and me dearly, often telling us he loved us, as he staggered drunkenly into our bedrooms at night to sit on our beds and attempt to give us fatherly knowledge. He always ended with professing his love for us, his two little girls and only children, who were being raised by his beloved mother, Ella Mae Fisher Fair from Dallas, Texas.

He loved us without a doubt, but he loved alcohol more. My father died when I was ten years old of alcohol-related illnesses like cirrhosis of the liver. While he was in my life for a short time, he did an excellent job of expressing his love for his children: Mary Aurelia and SaBrina Romania Fisher. His name was Jessie Paul Fisher, born in Dallas, Texas on February 28, His mother Ella Mae Fisher Fair and stepfather McClendon Fair brought him and his siblings to California for a better life. I know little about his childhood, but as an adult, he struggled with alcoholism.

I believe having substance abusers as parents kept me from ever abusing any substance. I avoided drugs at all costs. In my forties and fifties, I would enjoy a glass of red wine periodically, but I knew hard alcohol was off limits. I had no desire to be disorientated or out of control. At that time I believed I had a genetic predisposition to addiction, so the overuse of substances was not an option for me. Plus, I saw the horrific impact it had on families like mine and many others. Genetic markers may exist in families, but I believe our minds and strong God-given will have more power. Bottom line: humans are more powerful than they give themselves credit for. You do not have to follow in the footsteps of others just because you share the same blood. You can be just as determined as I was not to succumb to negative addictive vices. My main point is I had numerous reason to be mad at the world. With all that I had been through I easily could have used all my past trauma to act a complete fool and expect sympathy from the world. i chose differently and I want you to do the same.

Learning to be positive is a gift we can give ourselves. It is key in learning to master your emotions. It doesn't mean we are grinning from ear to ear daily and hopping around hugging random strangers and trees. It simply means learning to face each situation, assessing it, even if it is negative, and not allowing yourself to react in a way that causes you and others more pain and suffering. Look deeply into each moment and try to find the positive in it.

For example, imagine a young man showing up to work at a job he loves and has given his best to for over eight years. He is clearly next in line for the supervisor position, and today is the day it will be announced. He wears his best suit and tie, ready to accept his new position and get to work. During the meeting, the director calls a name that is not his. The director calls the name of a man who is hardworking and kind but, in the young man's opinion, not as qualified as he believes he is. He tries to keep his composure, but his heart is broken. He feels let down and overlooked.

These are the moments in life where circumstances seem negative. However, the young man's reaction does not have to be. He could scream, cry, and belittle the man that got the position. He could give a piece of his mind to the decision-makers. He could storm out, make a scene, and express his hurt and disappointment to all the employees. But that is not accessing the situation and finding the positive in it. That is not stopping, breathing, or thinking.

We can't always control the people around us, but we do have full control over our reactions to them. We can't control what happens in every situation because we cannot control other human beings. Maybe if the man who was passed over for the positive took a moment to detach from the emotional sting of it all and truly looked at all sides, he might have concluded that he could have done more. Perhaps his ego convinced him that he was putting in more effort and dedication at his job than he truly was. That doesn't have to be the case, but we need to learn to humble ourselves and look at both sides.

It's also possible that he was indeed the most qualified and that the position simply was not given to him. Even in cases like that, we still must maintain control. We can't allow our minds to tell us lies such as, "You aren't good enough." Putting ourselves down is never the answer. We also can't begin to have negative feelings about another person. We are all phenomenal, and each of us has special talents and gifts. Although it is common to attack ourselves when we get rejected and disappointed in life, continuing this mindset is very dangerous. We are all great and need to develop daily practices to invoke that feeling of greatness inside of us in all situations. There is no shortage of blessings. There is an abundance of blessings for us all. We must learn how to vibrate at the same frequency as them.

Anger and rage are a low-frequency emotions. Fear and self-doubt are also low frequencies. We can't allow our minds to wallow there. Even when we are hurt and disappointed, we must learn how to elevate our vibrations so that we can vibrate at the same frequency as the amazing blessings we desire in our life. Vibrating higher simply means, getting up and intentionally making yourself feel better. Use whatever tools work for you: get up and sing, laugh, dance, read, work out, pray, meditate, recite positive affirmations, whatever will lift your spirit. Do one or a combination of them all repeatedly. Eventually, it will become second nature and a regular part of your life, ensuring you maintain control of your emotions and live a better life than you would have otherwise.

As if staying positive itself wasn't already difficult. Imagine doing it when you have just been diagnosed with an illness. Picture yourself as a positive influencer, acclaimed for authoring the highly successful book titled *"Your Mind is Magic"*. However, you receive distressing news from your doctor: you have a tumor connected to your carotid artery. The surgical procedure to remove it presents two possible outcomes - it can either be a complete success, or a devastating failure resulting in permanent facial paralysis or immediate death due to excessive bleeding. How could one believe that staying positive is possible during times like these? Well, I'm here to convince you that it is. It's far from easy but possible. It requires daily commitment but it is indeed possible. Living in fear is not an option for me. I will enjoy life to the fullest no matter what. As I type this exact paragraph, I am on the Carnival Spirit Cruise ship enjoying a family vacation to Cozumel and Belize!

I have always worked out and maintained consistent exercise habits throughout my twenties, thirties, and forties. By the time I turned fifty on August 7, 2019, other than a few extra pounds and slightly higher than normal blood pressure, I felt I was in good shape. I went in for what was a standard tonsillectomy and adenoid removal surgery. There was also a small cyst in my ear that the doctor was going to remove as well. The tonsillectomy and adenoid surgery went perfectly.

However, when I woke up in recovery, Dr. McAlpin was standing at the foot of my bed, ready to inform me that when she entered through my ear to remove what she believed to be a small cyst, it bled profusely as soon as she made contact with it. She said she immediately realized it was not a cyst but a vascular tumor and informed me I would need another surgery. Over the next few months, I saw a neurosurgeon to prepare for the additional surgery, which was more serious than the initial surgery by the ear, nose, and throat specialist. By this time in my life, I was mastering positive thinking so much so that I had written several self-help books: *My Spiritual Smile: Tools for Mental and Emotional Transformation and Your Mind is Magic: A Guide to Maintaining Positive Thinking. Kicking Depression in the Butt: How to Battle the Internal Enemy and Win, How to Get*

Exactly What You Want From God: Mastering the Art of Effective Prayer, Despite the wonderful new positive mindset habits I had formed, I still had to do a lot of work to not succumb to fear after hearing the news. It was not easy, but it allowed me time to practice the positive tools I so very much believe in.

These tools helped me tackle those days when I did an Internet search on my tumor. These Internet searches would always produce pictures of people with the sides of their heads shaved and deep surgical scars from the front to the back of their heads. I even joined a few Facebook groups for people who had this exact type of tumor, which at the time they believed was an Acoustic Neuroma initially but later they settled on a Glomus Tympanicum. That decision to join that group was not a good idea. Being in the group kept me in a state of fear. Even once I had gotten to where I could resolve the feelings of fear, communicating with people who had unsuccessful surgeries and constantly seeing images of the aftermath and complications was not good for me. So, I left those groups alone.

By May 2023, after the COVID-19 pandemic canceled my scheduled surgery, I felt a twinge of pain in the area where the tumor was located. I created an affirmation for when I meditate. Each time I would feel the pain, instead of getting scared and worried, I would tell myself that the air I was breathing in was healing, restoring, and repairing every cell in my body. The air I was breathing out was releasing all toxins, sickness, and disease from my body. I convinced myself that the periodic pain was the tumor shrinking. This presents a challenge because it opposes logic. However, I strongly believe God has given us the power to heal our own bodies.

I was consistent with my "mindset magic" because I knew I had to reverse my way of thinking, but I knew it was possible.

Mindset magic is the phrase I use to refer to the amazing mental power we all possess, a powerful unseen force we can manipulate for the good. Some call that unseen positive force God. Some may refer to it in other ways. Don't get caught up in the words. Just know that everyone has access to that power; they simply have to tap into it. This amazing energy is also in the words we speak.

I had to adjust my affirmation from: "I Am Healing, Restoring, and Repairing" to "I Am Healed, Restored, and Repaired."It's already done! We must believe and thank God not for what we wish and pray will happen, but we must sustain the unshakable belief that it has already happened. It's a mindset twist, but it works. Believe in the unseen, and it will appear.

Just because a doctor has given us a prognosis doesn't mean we have to fall into a mindset of death and despair. Emotionally I wanted to scream and lose it. But That would have frighten my children and served no positive purpose. I am not saying to stifle normal hurt and disappointment. Cry, cry a river but eventually you must return to some semblance of emotional control. I still had to be a mother. I still had to go to work and pay the mortgage. I did just that. I used the tools I mention in this book to keep myself from drowning in fear.

I attended all of my scheduled appointments and followed all the doctors' orders, as I would advise everyone to do. However, in addition to that, I used visualization techniques to imagine the tumor getting smaller and smaller whenever I listened to this particular sound. The sound I chose was 432 Hz frequency. I learned about binaural beats many years prior and would periodically listen to 528 or 432 Hz binaural tones or Tibetan flute. I find it extremely peaceful and calming, making it perfect for meditation. Since it was familiar to me, I set an intention that every time I heard the tone, my tumor would shrink.

This type of visualization takes consistent work and, most importantly, a strong belief system. The logical mind, will attempt to talk us out of things that don't seem logical, but you must learn to bypass that and stay focused on the goal you are trying to achieve. Not every day will be a good day. On those days, it's especially important to implement the tools you're learning in this book. Some days, you may feel discouraged or have a hard time focusing. At times, it may feel silly, and you might think it's not working. Please do not give up. It takes repeatedly doing something for a while before it becomes a habit. Eventually, you will have practiced being positive so much that it will be a part of your authentic character. You are training your mind to look for the positive in all situations. You are trying to balance your emotions and it is not easy. Find tools as I did that help to keep you calm.

January 2025 almost five years later, my tumor was successfully removed at UCLA hospital in California by Dr. Akera Ishiyama with no major complications. God is Great.

There was a time when one of my adult children went missing. They had not made contact for days, and we were all worried. Although this was definitely cause for concern, in a situation like this, you still cannot allow your mind to take you down a dark road. As the days went by, I began to have thoughts of my child being found dead. I even had visions of being at their funeral. This was a very difficult time for me, but I knew the dangers of allowing myself to be so consumed with fear. I could not lose control of my emotions. I would not have been able to function for my other children. I tried to refrain from focusing on things that had not happened. I prayed and used my vibrational tools to keep me calm.

I understand that fear and worry can make you think horrible things, I get it. Negative thoughts will arise during crises like these, but you simply cannot allow them to linger. While my child was still missing, I consciously had to replace those negative images with positive ones. This is hard to do when you are overwhelmed with worry and concern, but I had to cast out the negative and replace it with the positive, or I would not have been able to get up in the morning. Three weeks later, we found my child alive. There were challenges that they still needed to face, but they were alive to face them. Had I given into those images of death, I believe it might have been different.

If that situation wasn't debilitating enough, a few years later, another one of my adult children went missing. Fortunately, by then, I was even more advanced in my positive thinking habits. After a few days of calling around and trying to piece things together, they were found in another state, though not in the best condition. As hard as that was to handle, I had to acknowledge the positive: they could have been dead. The phone call I received could have been to identify the body, but it wasn't, and for that, I was grateful.

Make no mistake, the conscious choice to stay positive in difficult situations doesn't always ease the pain or dismiss the reality of what's happening. In my case, it kept me from having a mental breakdown, which would have rendered me incapable of helping anyone. Pain is real, and certain life experiences can cause us tremendous suffering. However, if we train ourselves to stop for a moment, breathe, think and gain control of our emotions, we can manage it better. Focus on the thoughts you want to think about, not the uncontrollable ones fueled by fear. If you allow yourself that time, you're more likely to come up with the best solution for the problem. Those moments of silence and reflection can also help us accept the things we cannot change.

Although I know many parents have had to endure this disheartening experience, I do not believe God designed it for a parent to bury their child. Fortunately, despite some touch-and-go moments, as of 2024, all four of my beautiful children are alive and well, and I couldn't be more grateful.

We Are in Control

We must learn to control our emotions and reactions. No one can make you scream, holler, or lash out; you have full control over your behavior, even when someone provokes you and crosses a boundary. We live in a world with other human beings, and we cannot force our will onto them. Sometimes others are downright wrong in how they handle us, and we are justified in our hurt and anger. However, challenging or confronting them puts us in a negative headspace.

Sometimes, it is best to let it go, not only externally, but, most importantly, internally. Talking to yourself and having an imaginary conversation where you are telling the person off is just as damaging as actually confronting the person. Remember "What we think about, we bring about." If we hold on to anger, hostility, and resentment, we are the ones who suffer. We suffer mentally, physically and emotionally.

Internal peace and full control over ourselves is the desired result for us all. In some situations, addressing the person who has hurt, abused, or offended us is necessary and beneficial. However, it is vital to do this from a place of peace. Do not confront others while you are still angry or seeking vengeance. Some people have harmed us whom we may never see again, but we must release the pain associated with them and what they did to us. It is easier said than done, but it is crucial if we want to lead a happy, positive life and keep our minds free of negative thoughts.

Negativity will always exist in this world. There is nothing you can do to rid the world of negativity entirely. You cannot even appreciate the positive if you are unaware of the negative. This book helps you identify negative thoughts and replace them with positive ones. Darkness and light will always be factors in the world. Yin and Yang are realities of this world, no matter what. If only good existed, you would have no comparison. You can only identify good because you have seen and felt what bad is. You choose which area you want to operate in. Every day, you make a choice, even if you do not realize it. You are making a choice!

For example, one day, I had a tension headache, which is common. The week prior had been extremely busy, with long hours at my salon, plus a couple of women's seminars I attended. I also took my kids to the Monster Jam at the SoFi Stadium, which kept us up long past my desired bedtime. When I got the tension headache, instead of simply attributing it to the long, hard week before, I started thinking it was because the tumor in my head was growing. This could not have been further from the truth. I figured since I felt the pain on the left side, near my eye and ear where the tumor was, it certainly must be a side effect of the tumor's growth. This is a dangerous way to think, but these are exactly the examples of negative thinking I want you to identify after reading this book. Allowing yourself to think that way can surely cause your emotions to spiral.

I want you to learn how to "Catch and Cast" catch the negative thought as it comes in and cast it away. Replace it with a positive thought. I knew I had to cast those thoughts right out of my head, and I did. I took two Excedrin, went to bed, and felt wonderful the next day. Allowing myself to use the positive tool that I created kept me from loosing control of my emotions and becoming fearful that in some imminent danger from the tumor.

Identifying each time you slip into that dark-thinking place is the first step to winning the battle against negative thinking. When you notice the regularity of these negative thoughts, please do not feel defeated or disappointed in yourself. Instead, applaud the fact that you can now recognize and control when it is happening. If you do not notice the negative thoughts, you cannot change them into positive ones. Consider it growth that you can notice when your thought pattern has taken a turn for the worse. We can all lead predominantly positive lives, which will allow us to enjoy this beautiful life experience to the fullest. It all begins in our minds,master your thoughts, and you will master your life.

Every day may present a circumstance that can upset you, but you can handle anything. If you are still reading this book then you know that you are the one in control of your emotion and reactions. One day, I took my middle daughter to the dentist. While waiting for her in the car, I used that time to get some writing done on this very book. I knew better than to let the radio play while the car was off, so I did not have the radio on. I waited for about an hour and a half, and when she was done, I attempted to start the car, but the ignition would not start.

The car's computer system had been telling me to replace the battery in my car key, for weeks, but I had not made time to do that because the dealership was far from my home, and I do not like driving distances. It was nearing 10:30 a.m., and I had to be at work at my salon by 1:00 p.m. I started to get annoyed. Then I remembered that all Mercedes-Benz cars come with free roadside assistance for life. I called them, and although it took them about an hour, they came out and started the car.

While waiting, I took a few deep breaths and pushed down the anxious feeling of annoyance when they tried to rise up. I crawled into the back seat and began writing this very paragraph. These are the daily life episodes where we must learn to remain positive. I filled my mind with all the positives in this situation. It could have been much closer to the time I needed to be at work, which would have made me late. It could have been nighttime instead of 10:00 a.m., which would have been frightening for my daughter and I to be stranded at night. I might not have been blessed with free roadside assistance and could have been stranded with my daughter without a plan. It could have been a much worse situation.

It may not always seem like it, but there is a positive in every situation. Sometimes small inconveniences, such as my car not starting up, force us to slow down and take care of important things we may be neglecting. I knew for over a month that the battery in my car key remote was very low. The funny thing is, I had no idea the computer in the car and the computer in the key needed to work together for the car to start. Mercedes Roadside Assistance came right out, started my vehicle, and then my daughter and I drove straight to the dealer, got the new car key batteries, and even picked up a couple of cute Mercedes caps while I was there. All things work out for the good.

I have been in many relationships that have led me to develop negative feelings. When you give your heart, mind, body, and soul to another person and they mistreat you, it can indeed put you in a very negative place. Staying in that dark place can cause you to react in ways that are not productive. Sometimes, we cannot believe the audacity of people who do cruel and disloyal things, especially when we feel we have been good to them. I know firsthand how painful these situations can be.

I have lost control many times when I felt betrayed by a lover, spouse, or even a family member. However, a negative, explosive reaction never produces a good result. While there may be momentary satisfaction, in the long run, you end up feeling worse about yourself for how you responded, which only causes you more pain and suffering. Your reaction does not change the other person's behavior, so it is pointless.

We have all been hurt by others but we still have to learn to control our emotions. The emotions will pass, no matter how extreme they may seem in the moment, and eventually, the situation will not seem so dire. The pain will subside, trust me, it will. We must learn to remember that, even amid negativity, positive things still exist. Be patient with yourself, because all wombs will heal.

I was once one of those hurt people who lashed out when I was in pain. However, there is a better way. There is a way to handle pain and disappointment that will not make you feel horrible about yourself and will not cause another person the very pain you do not want to feel. When someone hurts your feelings, insults you or betrays your love and loyalty, stop and take a breath. Acknowledge how it made you feel. Give yourself time to process and allow those feelings to pass. They will, even though it may seem like they will last forever, they will not.

If you must address the situation, do so calmly and with a level head. Handle it in a way that does not inflict pain on another person. Returning to a place of love does not mean you have to continue engaging with the person or that you are still in love with them. It means you love yourself enough to react in a way that fosters love, not hate. You will always feel better in the end when you choose the positive over the negative. Hate, resentment, and anger can lead to sickness and disease in the body. Remember, positivity is not about perfection. It is about learning to stay positive even when life is not perfect, and that effort is worth it.

We can have a better world despite how horrible things may seem. Yes, hate, greed, crime, sickness, and death exist, along with a host of other horrific things. Yes, unnecessary wars are being fought all over the world, claiming the lives of many innocent people. However, even amid global catastrophes, you can still choose to focus on the positive. It does not make you a bad person to enjoy life while others are suffering from poverty and death. Those harsh realities will always exist, but we do not have to stay focused on them. The bad will always be there, but so will the good. Focus all your energy on the things that make you smile. Find positive tools that help keep you uplifted and in control of your emotions.

10

You Win The War

It's time to celebrate your new life where you are the master of your fate! Learning how to control your thoughts and emotions is the catalyst to that. This is the beginning of a great life. It's all uphill from here. If you utilize the positive mind tools I speak of in the book, you absolutely cannot fail. You can win the war against negative thinking and impulsive behavior every single time. You have a magnificent future ahead of you. I am excited for you. Let every new season in your life be a winning season. Winning the battle over negative thinking and maintaining full control over all of your emotions will be one of the most significant and useful skills to have mastered. It will change your life.

It's one thing to learn to win the war against negative thinking yourself. It is a whole different challenge to teach it to others. However, that is exactly what it will take in order for the generations that follow us to be empowered enough to make an impactful difference in the world. We must teach each child about the infinite power within themselves. they must learn to stop, breath and think before they react.

I have four children who thankfully got to be around during my mindset transformation and reaped the benefits of having a person in the home with them daily who was attempting to master the practice of positive thinking, thus being able to teach it to them. I am certain that even during times when they appeared to be disinterested, the concepts and ideas still rubbed off on them a bit. Their wonderful, expansive minds are like soil. If we plant positive thoughts, ideas, and concepts into them regularly, they will eventually develop habitual behaviors that will make them better people. My children, as well as yours, will have to create their own path, but I pray that watching me diligently follow my path shows my children that it is possible. All things are possible.

At age fifty-four, I began painting again. I always had the desire and the talent to paint, but I was so busy running "Braids By SaBrina" and "A New Vision Dreadlock Studio" and teaching braiding and dreadlock classes that I simply did not have time to paint. I had literally forgotten that I loved painting. It was only when I slowed my life down that I remembered the things that I was truly passionate about and began painting again. I painted just for myself, and it was gratifying and peaceful.

One day, after watching a video of me painting on TikTok, a woman named Maria kept asking if she could buy one of my paintings. Since I had never even considered selling them, I told her no. She asked a second and maybe even a third time. Suddenly, a little light bulb turned on, and I agreed to sell her the painting. That was all it took for me to tap into that "Inspiration for creation" and turn my passion into profit. I quickly created about fifteen paintings. I called them "Spiritual Art From My Heart." I created a website and all other social media forums, and Whoa La! A new business was born. In the first seven days, I had already sold four paintings. I shifted into the energy of what I call "Creation Mode." When in creation mode, ideas are constantly flowing freely. You can't sleep until you complete your new project or, as I sometimes say, "Until you give birth to the new idea." We have all felt the powerful energy of "Creation Mode," but sometimes our daily lives distract us from recognizing it.

I urge anyone who can identify when they are operating at a high level of vibration to seize those moments and try to zero in on what God is trying to tell you to create. This is the energy that builds businesses. It's the solution energy, where you will always seem to find the answer to whatever you are seeking. It's fast-paced and quick because it's passing through you. You must grab it and relish in the feeling. Write every thought down, and meditate more often when you are feeling this magnificent energy. It will not last. It is a fleeting energy, far too powerful to exist indefinitely.

This energetic zone is the epitome of what I mean by the title of chapter nine, "Vibrate High." It is God within you, pushing you towards your purpose. You will experience little bursts of it throughout your entire life. Use those to your advantage. All of us have something amazing that God wants us to bring to fruition.

Sometimes tragedy or challenging situations can invoke that creative energy as well. When my youngest daughter was ten years old, in the fourth and fifth grades, we had a situation where she was being bullied. It was quite hurtful because the other child was her best friend. Well, her BFF (Best Friend Forever), as they call it. As soon as I became aware of the situation, I immediately contacted the school and the other child's primary parent. Unfortunately, the parent of the bully was dismissive and made excuses for her child's behavior. The mother seemed to be of a similar mindset. After several meetings with the school principal and the teachers and counselors at the school, I became extremely frustrated and concerned about my daughter's emotional stability. Although removing her from school was an option, I did not believe that would fix the problem. There are bullies everywhere, in schools, workplaces, and even in the home.

Out of my frustration, I decided to create a positive movement for children to teach them how to navigate negative conversations, how to uplift themselves and others, and how to gain the strength and courage to say, "No, you cannot treat me like that." We must teach our children that it is okay to speak up for themselves, even if they are afraid. Three days into my daughter's fifth-grade year, I had an appointment with the school to further address the fact that bad behavior from the same female student in fourth grade had carried over and was already beginning in the fifth grade. I thought it was important for the principal and teachers to be informed about this, hoping that they would finally address the behavior of this specific child. My patience was wearing thin with the school, but since I agreed to meet them the next morning at 8:15 a.m., I sat down and tapped into that creative spirit of mine and created "The Positive Crew System."

My computer printer wasn't working properly, so I went across the street to my godmother's house to use her computer and printer. I made about eight copies and took them with me to school the next morning. I even made a mission statement and an oath for the children to learn. I videotaped my daughter and her friend reciting the oath. I even had my best friend's grandson make a video. It was a fun way to introduce positivity to elementary school-age children.

I am learning to be in tune with when the power of God moves through me. I recognize that amazing energy because when it is active, ideas are instantaneous. This is the oath I created in five minutes:

The Positive Crew Oath

I am part of the Positive Crew And negativity, we just don't do!
We uplift ourselves and others. Every day of the week
We only use nice words when we speak I will be kind to every boy
and girl
So, we all can have a better world

If I'm completely honest, I never had any strong urges to work with children. I love kids and even have plans to write a children's book, but I never felt compelled to create and design a motivational program specifically for kids before that day. That's why I believe it was God pushing me for another purpose He had for my life.

I went on to create a mission statement and a page filled with other ideas of what this newfound Positive Crew System could develop into. Bullying is a nationwide problem. Children can only benefit from learning to be kinder to each other. We have nothing to lose. "The Positive Crew System" will teach them specific short, memorable phrases to navigate out of negative, hurtful conversations. It will teach them how to choose to say something nice as opposed to something hurtful. It will make being positive a cool thing. The mental health of the little people we depend on to evolve humanity for the better is at stake.

The point of this story is to get you to understand that you must always stop, take a breath, and try to find the positive in all situations. I was mad and frustrated with the child and the school. Had I responded out of that anger and frustration, the school would have never let me in the door, let alone listened to my proposal for "The Positive Crew System."

Even when we practice maintaining positivity, the ups and downs of life can still affect us. Don't feel you have failed. Positivity is a daily practice. However, I believe that we all stand a better chance of this world changing for the better if we empower children while they are young and impressionable. They truly are our future, so let's make sure they grow up armed with the tools needed to win the wars they will encounter throughout their lives.

There will always be opportunities in life for you to choose positivity. We are human beings, so we will never be immune to feelings of hurt and disappointment. However, when we choose to handle them positively, we will find that each time we learn a lesson that will assist us in our own emotional evolution. We become better people when we learn to respond from a place of love. Love is our true nature.

Make no mistake, there are people who will challenge us. For example, I have a friend who is part of "The Order Of the Eastern Stars," an organization I am a proud member of. She and I clicked immediately. She is funny, and no matter how long we go without seeing each other, we always fall right back into hysterical laughter when we get together.

In February 2024, she came back to California to tend to her ailing mother's needs. We met up the next day at an event. I was thrilled, as usual, to see her. I ran straight to her when she entered the room and gave her a big hug. She instantly began comically insulting me. As we posed for a picture, she said, "Hold your stomach in." I said, "You hold yours in," which is something I would never say to anyone. As we were leaving, she hugged me and said, "Bye, Chunky," alluding to the fact that I had gained weight. This time, I simply said, "I look fabulous."

It absolutely hurt my feelings, but what was most hurtful was, as my two daughters and I drove home, my older daughter JJ said, "Don't let her hurt your feelings, Mom. She was being mean." I had no idea they heard her. I explained to them that no one, especially a friend whom I am first in line to support, should ever treat someone that way. She, too, had gained weight, but I would never have pointed it out to her or anyone. This is prime example of moments where you need to exercise emotional control. The old me, the person who had not spent years healing and training myself to have full control would have started slinging insults, much worse than the one comment I did hurl back at her. the old me would have completely lost control because of my hurt feelings and I would have felt horrible later.

I should never have allowed her to pull me into that negativity. When I snapped back at her, "Hold your stomach in" comment with "Hold yours in, too," that was wrong and goes against everything I believe in. I realized at that moment that possibly our friendship had run its course. If I am honest with myself, she has always been that way. She has always been a mean girl. I loved her so dearly that I chose to ignore it. But at this stage in my life, I was not willing to allow anyone to insult me.

Absolutely, I may have been extra sensitive because I had gained more weight than I desired. Maybe when I became her friend thirteen years earlier, I could engage in some negative conversations about others with her. But I was no longer that person. I had grown past that level of immaturity and was proud of my growth. I had won the war against the enemy of my mind. It saddened me that she still had not at sixty years old. However, we all have our own journeys. We all evolve at different paces.

She did call me about an hour later, but she was completely oblivious to the fact that her words were hurtful. I told her that my daughters heard her and had to comfort me when they realized her words hurt my feelings. She brushed it off by saying, "Girl, I talk about myself being fat all the time." No accountability whatsoever. I was a little sad because I knew it would be the end of the friendship as we once knew it. I'll always be cordial, and we may exchange a laugh or two when she comes to town, but that will be it. And that is okay. We can indeed love people from a distance. Every hurtful situation does not have to result in a negative confrontation.

I would not want my daughters to allow any friend to treat them that way. However i also want them to see and example of emotional control. Sometimes people who trigger us and put us in those positions have to be left in the past. I wish her the absolute best in life, and I'm trying hard not to judge her because this is not new behavior for her. However, it is behavior I refuse to tolerate from anyone, especially from those who claim to love me. Friends uplift and encourage each other. Friends don't take potshots at each other for laughs.

There was a time when I was so broken that I would never have had the strength to distance myself from a hurtful friend. I did not love myself wholeheartedly then.

I'm not mad at my friend. I love her to this day. I pray for her regularly, but the only person that can change her is her. That holds true for each one of us. If there are behaviors or personality traits that you are not proud of, change them. Only you can create a better you. Each of us individually working on ourselves leads to humanity as a whole changing for the better collectively.

That moment could have ended very differently. A few careless words. A wounded ego. A flash of anger. One explosion. Then suddenly the story would no longer be about growth, it would be about regret. That is how quickly lives are altered when emotions are not under control. That is how fast damage is done when we allow our emotions take the lead instead of wisdom.

This is what *How Do I Control My Emotions?* is truly about. Not perfection or pretending you don't feel pain. But learning how to stop a moment from becoming a mistake. Learning how to pause long enough to protect your future from your feelings.

Every single day, life presents us with opportunities to react in a negative way. Someone says something careless. Someone disrespects us. Someone hurts our feelings. Someone touches an old wound we thought had healed. In those moments, we are standing at a crossroads. One path leads to escalation, destruction, and regret. The other leads to self-control, dignity, and peace.

The truth is, reacting rarely fixes anything. It may feel powerful in the moment, but it often costs us relationships, opportunities, freedom, and sometimes even lives. There are prisons filled with people who reacted instead of paused. There are cemeteries filled because someone could not control their anger for five seconds. That is not an exaggeration, that is reality.

As adults, we must learn this lesson. More importantly, we must teach it to our children. We cannot continue passing down unchecked rage, impulsive behavior, and emotional immaturity and then wonder why the world looks the way it does. Emotional control is not weakness. It is survival. It is leadership and love in action.

That day, I did not win because I looked fabulous. I won because I did not allow my hurt feeling to make me explode. I won because I chose restraint over retaliation. I won because my daughters witnessed a woman feel hurt, and still choose control. That is what winning the war looks like. Not the absence of pain, but mastery over it.

You will be hurt in life. People will make you angry. That is unavoidable. What *is* avoidable is what you do next. You always have a choice. You can react, or you can respond. You can let anger lead, or you can lead yourself.

If you take nothing else from this book, take this: controlling your emotions does not mean suppressing them. It means honoring them without letting them destroy you. It means choosing who you want to be in the moment that matters most.

When you learn how to control your emotions, you don't just change your life, you protect it, and that is how you win the war.

About the Author

SaBrina Fisher Reece understands what it means to keep going without applause.

For over twenty-six years, she built one of the most influential braiding salons and schools in Los Angeles-**Braids By SaBrina**-earning recognition throughout California as "The Braid Queen." Her name was on the door, her reputation on the line, and her success was self-made. But behind the achievements was a quieter truth: much of her journey was navigated without consistent support, validation, or encouragement from others.

SaBrina's life has been shaped by early abandonment, profound loss, and hard-earned self-trust. Those experiences taught her that confidence on the outside does not always mean peace on the inside, and that real strength is learned when you are forced to become your own support system.

Today, SaBrina is an author, speaker, and guide focused on emotional growth, self-mastery, and inner alignment. She is the author of several transformational works, including *My Spiritual Smile, Your Mind Is Magic, Perfectly Positive, Living Life on a Higher Frequency, How to Get Exactly What You Want From God,*

Kicking Depression in the Butt, Become Your own Cheerleader, Family Fun Night Cookbook, When I Say "I Am", and How to Make More Money in 2026. Each reflects a chapter of her own evolution.

Now residing in New Mexico, SaBrina continues her work through writing, sound-based healing practices and helping others bring their literary dreams to print through **In59Seconds Publishing Co.** She is always reminding readers that there is no single path to peace, only the courage to walk your own.

Her message is simple and unwavering: Sometimes the most important applause you will ever receive is the one you give yourself.

You can connect with me on:

🜨 https://in59secondspublishing.com

⬛ https://www.facebook.com/InspireMeBri

Also by SaBrina Fisher Reece

Become Your Own Cheerleader

Become Your Own Cheerleader: Moving Forward in Life Without the Support of Others is a powerful, honest guide for anyone who has ever felt unseen, unsupported, or overlooked by the very people they hoped would cheer the loudest.

In this deeply personal and transformational book, SaBrina Fisher Reece invites readers into her life story, one shaped by early abandonment, profound loss, resilience, and hard-earned self-trust. From surviving childhood trauma and the murder of the grandmother who raised her, to building businesses, writing books, and leading without consistent support, SaBrina reveals what happens when you stop waiting for applause and start standing firmly in your own worth.

This is not a book about bitterness. It is a book about liberation.

Through raw storytelling and hard truths, you will learn why some people cannot clap for you, how to stop taking silence personally, and why your worth is never up for a vote. You will discover how to release the need for validation, acknowledge the few who truly support you, and become the voice you once needed to hear from others.

Each chapter builds toward one essential truth: the most powerful support you will ever receive must come from within.

Whether you are navigating family disappointment, friendship distance, professional invisibility, or emotional independence, **Become Your Own Cheerleader** offers clarity, comfort, and courage. It teaches you how to keep going when no one is watching, how to celebrate yourself without guilt, and how to live boldly without waiting for permission.

This book is for the strong ones who got strong too early.

For the ones who kept showing up.

For the ones who learned how to clap for themselves.

If you are ready to stop waiting for approval and start living like you believe in you, this book is for you.

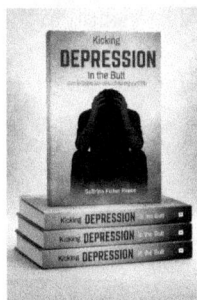

Kicking Depression In the Butt

Kicking Depression in the Butt is a raw, faith-infused, and deeply practical guide for anyone who is tired of surviving in silence and ready to reclaim their life.

Drawing from her own lived experiences with trauma, abandonment, loss, and depression, SaBrina Fisher Reece invites readers into an honest conversation about what depression really feels like, and how to fight back. This book does not minimize pain or offer shallow positivity. Instead, it helps readers recognize depression as an internal enemy, interrupt destructive thought cycles, and rebuild their inner world with intention, truth, and daily tools that actually work.

Through personal storytelling, spiritual insight, and mindset-shifting strategies, SaBrina shows readers how to stop identifying with their darkest thoughts and begin designing a life that protects their peace. She addresses the realities of trauma, triggers, boundaries, faith, therapy, medication, and personal responsibility, offering a balanced approach that honors both professional support and inner work.

Kicking Depression in the Butt is for the person who keeps showing up while quietly falling apart. It is for those who smile while suffering, who feel strong on the outside but exhausted on the inside. Most of all, it is a reminder that depression may visit, but it does not get to stay, and it does not get to become your identity.

This book is not about perfection. It's about progress. It's about learning how to fight for your mind, your peace, and your future, one thought, one choice, and one day at a time.

Because as long as you have breath in your body, your story is not over—and you still have the power to kick depression in the butt.

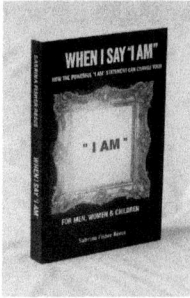

When I Say "I AM"

When I Say " I AM"

What you say after "I Am" has the power to shape your entire life.

In *When I Say "I Am"*, SaBrina Fisher Reece reveals the sacred and scientific power of spoken identity. Blending spiritual truth, biblical wisdom, and universal law, this transformational book teaches readers how their words are not just communication, but creation. Every "I Am" statement becomes a command to the subconscious, a signal to the universe, and a declaration to the spiritual realm.

Drawing from scripture, including God's revelation of "I AM" as the eternal source of being, SaBrina shows how the same creative force lives within each of us. Through emotionally moving insight, practical affirmations, and deep spiritual awareness, readers learn how to shift from fear-based language to faith-based declarations that activate healing, confidence, abundance, and purpose.

This book will help you:

Break negative identity patterns

Reprogram limiting beliefs

Speak life instead of fear

Align your words with divine promise

Use "I Am" as a daily tool for transformation

More than motivation, *When I Say "I Am"* is a blueprint for conscious creation. It reminds you that your voice is powerful, your identity is sacred, and your words are always working, either for you or against you.

If you are ready to stop speaking survival and start speaking destiny, this book will show you how to command your life with intention, faith, and divine authority, one "I Am" at a time.

Family Fun Night Cookbook

Family Fun Night Cookbook is more than a collection of recipes, it's a simple, joyful way to bring families back together in the kitchen.

Designed for **kids, teens, and young adults**, this cookbook features **60 easy, safe, and family-approved recipes** that turn everyday meals into meaningful moments. Whether your children are little helpers, teenagers learning independence, or young adults home from college for the holidays, these recipes invite everyone to participate, contribute, and connect.

Cooking together builds more than meals. It builds confidence, communication, patience, and teamwork. This book encourages children of all ages to develop life skills while strengthening family bonds through shared experiences. The recipes are intentionally simple, approachable, and fun, making it easy for busy families to slow down and enjoy time together without stress.

Inside, you'll find meals that work for weeknights, weekends, holidays, and family gatherings, recipes that spark conversation, laughter, and a sense of togetherness. Each dish is crafted to be safe and accessible, allowing kids to help in age-appropriate ways while parents feel confident and relaxed.

In a world that moves fast and pulls families in different directions, **Family Fun Night Cookbook** creates space for connection. It turns cooking into collaboration. It transforms the kitchen into a place of learning, love, and lasting memories.

This is not about perfection. It's about presence.

It's about putting phones down, pulling chairs up, and making memories one recipe at a time.

If you're looking for a simple way to strengthen relationships, teach valuable life skills, and enjoy meaningful time together, this cookbook belongs in your home.

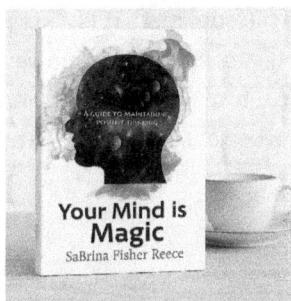

✧ YOUR MIND IS MAGIC - Discover the Power Already Within You ✧

By SaBrina Fisher Reece

What if the life you desire isn't something you have to chase... but something you can *create*?

In **Your Mind Is Magic**, SaBrina Fisher Reece, entrepreneur, author, and transformational speaker, reveals the extraordinary truth that most people never learn: **your thoughts are your greatest creative tool.** You are a limitless being with the God-given ability to shape your reality from the inside out.

This inspiring, practical guide teaches you how to harness the spiritual and energetic power of your own mind so you can finally live the life you *know* is meant for you.

✧ Inside This Book, You Will Learn How To:

✔ Reprogram your daily thoughts to support joy, peace, and success

✔ Break negative mental habits and replace them with powerful new patterns

✔ Activate your inner "Mind Magic" to attract love, abundance, health, and opportunity

✔ Align your energy with the life you desire

✔ Build a mindset of gratitude, confidence, and emotional freedom

✔ Use the Law of Assumption, visualization, and spiritual self-mastery to transform your world

✧ A Daily Guide for Becoming the Highest Version of Yourself

Your Mind Is Magic isn't just a motivational read, it is a **step-by-step roadmap** to mental, emotional, and spiritual empowerment. Every chapter gives you practical tools, reflections, and vibrational techniques to help you think better... feel better... and *live better.*

You will learn how to:
- Shift your frequency
- Protect your energy
- Speak powerfully
- Create new beliefs
- Heal old wounds
- Manifest with intention

And consciously design a life filled with **happiness, love, wealth, and wellness**

✧ For Anyone Ready to Take Control of Their Life

Whether you are healing from past pain, overcoming fear, rebuilding your confidence, or stepping into a new chapter, this book offers the encouragement and clarity you need to rise.

Your thoughts are portals.

Your words are spells.

Your mind is magic,

and this book shows you exactly how to use it.

www.ingramcontent.com/pod-product-compliance
Lightning Source LLC
LaVergne TN
LVHW051810080426
835513LV00017B/1891